Bipolar Disorder

Other Books in the Social Issues Firsthand Series:

AIDS

Blended Families

Bullying

Child Abuse and Neglect

Date and Acquaintance Rape

Disasters

Drunk Driving

Eating Disorders

Juvenile Crime

Mixed Heritage

Prostitution

Sexual Predators

Teenage Pregnancy

Web 2.0

SOCIAL ISSUES
FIRSTHAND

Bipolar Disorder

Stefan Kiesbye, Book Editor

GREENHAVEN PRESS
A part of Gale, Cengage Learning

GALE
CENGAGE Learning

Detroit • New York • San Francisco • New Haven, Conn • Waterville, Maine • London

GALE
CENGAGE Learning

Christine Nasso, *Publisher*
Elizabeth Des Chenes, *Managing Editor*

For more information, contact:
Greenhaven Press
27500 Drake Rd.
Farmington Hills, MI 48331-3535
Or you can visit our Internet site at gale.cengage.com

Articles in Greenhaven Press anthologies are often edited for length to meet page requirements. In addition, original titles of these works are changed to clearly present the main thesis and to explicitly indicate the author's opinion. Every effort is made to ensure that Greenhaven Press accurately reflects the original intent of the authors. Every effort has been made to trace the owners of copyrighted material.

Cover photograph © Louie Psihoyos/Science Faction/Corbis.

LIBRARY OF CONGRESS CATALOGING-IN-PUBLICATION DATA

Bipolar disorder / Stefan Kiesbye, book editor.
   p. cm. -- (Social issues firsthand)
   Includes bibliographical references and index.
   ISBN 978-0-7377-4658-7 (hardcover)
   1. Manic-depressive illness. I. Kiesbye, Stefan.
   RC516.B57 2010
   616.89'5--dc22

                                                      2009038624

Printed in the United States of America
1 2 3 4 5 6 7 13 12 11 10 09

Contents

Foreword   **9**

Introduction   **12**

Chapter 1: Living with Bipolar Disorder

1. Being Diagnosed with Bipolar Disorder   **16**
   at the Age of Fifteen

   Patrick Jamieson

   When diagnosed as a teenager, the author finds that there
   are no books on the illness available for adolescents, and
   later in adulthood sets out to chronicle his affliction
   from a teenage perspective.

2. What It Feels Like to Live with Bipolar Disorder   **28**

   Jane Pauley, interviewed by Patrick Perry

   Broadcast journalist Jane Pauley talks about her diagnosis
   of bipolar disorder at age 50, and how it has affected her
   life.

3. Not Sick Enough to Be Hospitalized   **32**

   Anonymous

   A woman with bipolar disorder and borderline personality disorder seeks to be voluntarily hospitalized, but cannot receive help, because she does not appear "crazy"
   enough.

4. A Pregnant Woman Lives Through   **41**
   Postpartum Psychosis

   Bipolar Chica

   After a difficult pregnancy, a woman with bipolar disorder experiences rage and the urge to harm her newborn.

5. Coming to Terms with Being Bipolar   **46**

   Anna Pearce and Matt Scanlon

   Actress Patty Duke discusses her childhood struggles
   with anxiety and depression that became full bipolar disorder in her teens.

6. In the Grip of Ups and Downs   53

Ryan Christman

In this personal essay, the author describes the rampant thoughts and desperate behavior he experiences. Step by step he leads the reader through the labyrinth of depressive moods and restlessness.

Chapter 2: Coping with a Loved One's Bipolar Disorder

1. My Dad's Disorder   59

Becky Aarons

A seventh-grade girl writes about her father's disorder.

2. My Wife Is Bipolar   62

Kenneth Richard Fox

The writer talks about his wife's violent assaults, resulting in the end of their marriage.

3. Raising a Child with Bipolar Disorder   70

Debbie Orkin

A mother discusses the daily challenges of raising her son, who has bipolar disorder.

4. Our Marriage Became Constant Chaos   79

Y. Euny Hong

Believing she has found the love of her life, the writer marries a charming, spontaneous man only to discover that he is suffering from bipolar disorder.

5. Dating a Bipolar Woman   85

Justin Clark

Attracted to the vibrant energy of his date, the author falls in love with her because of her bipolar disorder and not despite it. But soon their life together becomes defined by her obsessive need for routines and her illness, until there is no space left for anything else.

Chapter 3: Treating Bipolar Disorder

1. Medications Can Wreak Havoc on Your   94
Mind and Body
Pole to Polar

A woman details her struggle to treat her bipolar disorder. While several medications bring short-term relief from some symptoms, they often exacerbate others.

2. A Change in Diet and Exercise Improved   100
My Bipolar Symptoms
Karl

The writer describes how changing his exercise and eating habits lessened the effects of his once violent ups and downs.

3. Not All Children with Behavior Problems   108
Need Medication
Laurel Williams

A psychiatrist uses a real-world example to demonstrate that too many children are diagnosed with bipolar disorder, and parents too often listen to promises made by pharmaceutical ads.

4. Thyroid Hormones Help Treat Bipolar Disorder   112
Peter Whybrow, interviewed by the Saturday Evening Post

Peter Whybrow discusses the benefits of using thyroid hormones to treat bipolar disorder.

Organizations to Contact   123

For Further Research   127

Index   132

Foreword

Social issues are often viewed in abstract terms. Pressing challenges such as poverty, homelessness, and addiction are viewed as problems to be defined and solved. Politicians, social scientists, and other experts engage in debates about the extent of the problems, their causes, and how best to remedy them. Often overlooked in these discussions is the human dimension of the issue. Behind every policy debate over poverty, homelessness, and substance abuse, for example, are real people struggling to make ends meet, to survive life on the streets, and to overcome addiction to drugs and alcohol. Their stories are ubiquitous and compelling. They are the stories of everyday people—perhaps your own family members or friends—and yet they rarely influence the debates taking place in state capitols, the national Congress, or the courts.

The disparity between the public debate and private experience of social issues is well illustrated by looking at the topic of poverty. Each year the U.S. Census Bureau establishes a poverty threshold. A household with an income below the threshold is defined as poor, while a household with an income above the threshold is considered able to live on a basic subsistence level. For example, in 2003 a family of two was considered poor if its income was less than $12,015; a family of four was defined as poor if its income was less than $18,810. Based on this system, the bureau estimates that 35.9 million Americans (12.5 percent of the population) lived below the poverty line in 2003, including 12.9 million children below the age of eighteen.

Commentators disagree about what these statistics mean. Social activists insist that the huge number of officially poor Americans translates into human suffering. Even many families that have incomes above the threshold, they maintain, are likely to be struggling to get by. Other commentators insist

9

that the statistics exaggerate the problem of poverty in the United States. Compared to people in developing countries, they point out, most so-called poor families have a high quality of life. As stated by journalist Fidelis Iyebote, "Cars are owned by 70 percent of 'poor' households. . . . Color televisions belong to 97 percent of the 'poor' [and] videocassette recorders belong to nearly 75 percent. . . . Sixty-four percent have microwave ovens, half own a stereo system, and over a quarter possess an automatic dishwasher."

However, this debate over the poverty threshold and what it means is likely irrelevant to a person living in poverty. Simply put, poor people do not need the government to tell them whether they are poor. They can see it in the stack of bills they cannot pay. They are aware of it when they are forced to choose between paying rent or buying food for their children. They become painfully conscious of it when they lose their homes and are forced to live in their cars or on the streets. Indeed, the written stories of poor people define the meaning of poverty more vividly than a government bureaucracy could ever hope to. Narratives composed by the poor describe losing jobs due to injury or mental illness, depict horrific tales of childhood abuse and spousal violence, recount the loss of friends and family members. They evoke the slipping away of social supports and government assistance, the descent into substance abuse and addiction, the harsh realities of life on the streets. These are the perspectives on poverty that are too often omitted from discussions over the extent of the problem and how to solve it.

Greenhaven Press's *Social Issues Firsthand* series provides a forum for the often-overlooked human perspectives on society's most divisive topics of debate. Each volume focuses on one social issue and presents a collection of ten to sixteen narratives by those who have had personal involvement with the topic. Extra care has been taken to include a diverse range of perspectives. For example, in the volume on adoption, readers will find the stories of birth parents who have made an adoption plan, adoptive parents, and adoptees themselves. After exposure to these varied points of view, the reader will have a clearer understanding that adoption is an intense, emotional experience full of joyous highs and painful lows for all concerned.

The debate surrounding embryonic stem cell research illustrates the moral and ethical pressure that the public brings to bear on the scientific community. However, while nonexperts often criticize scientists for not considering the potential negative impact of their work, ironically the public's reaction against such discoveries can produce harmful results as well. For example, although the outcry against embryonic stem cell research in the United States has resulted in fewer embryos being destroyed, those with Parkinson's, such as actor Michael J. Fox, have argued that prohibiting the development of new stem cell lines ultimately will prevent a timely cure for the disease that is killing Fox and thousands of others.

Each book in the series contains several features that enhance its usefulness, including an in-depth introduction, an annotated table of contents, bibliographies for further research, a list of organizations to contact, and a thorough index. These elements—combined with the poignant voices of people touched by tragedy and triumph—make the *Social Issues Firsthand* series a valuable resource for research on today's topics of political discussion.

Introduction

Chase Edwards, a 12-year-old boy in Michigan, had been a seemingly healthy boy, when he suddenly became "irritable and apathetic," writes Kara Gavin for the University of Michigan Health System Newsroom. "He had trouble sleeping. He had complained of frequent stomachaches. . . . He dropped out of sports and school government. His parents didn't know it, but his drawings and a school essay hinted at the despair that was eating him up from the inside." Chase succumbed to that despair, committing suicide a few weeks before his thirteenth birthday.

His family and his teachers didn't put the clues together while Chase was still alive. But it all became clear after he died. "I never thought Chase was depressed, and the reason I didn't is because I had no idea of what depression was," says [his father] Jeff. "Kids don't come with instructions, and there are some things you don't know. But what's worse is that there are some things you don't *know* that you don't know about." Chase's father didn't know about depression and the closely related bipolar disorder (also known as manic depression), which are among the main causes of suicide and suicide attempts by adolescents.

Another young victim of a mood disorder, Garrett Smith, killed himself a day before his twenty-second birthday. His note read, "Dear family and friends, I have wanted to do this for years. There will most likely be a lot of people who will wonder why, but just not understand. The one thing I have done is given up. I can't handle it anymore. . . ." Garrett, the son of Senator Gordon Smith, is suspected to have had bipolar disorder. Before his suicide, he saw a psychiatrist who prescribed an antidepressant—a type of medication not recommended for this affliction. His family had noted his bouts of what his father described as "dangerous mental darkness," but they had not known that Garrett suffered from bipolar disorder. The student at Utah Valley State College had met with counselors and therapists, but he found little relief and ultimately didn't have the strength to continue.

According to the Society for Neuroscience in *Brain Research Success Stories*, "an estimated 2.3 million Americans are living with bipolar disorder," and both men and women are equally afflicted. Without appropriate treatment, "bipolar disorder has a suicide rate of up to 19 percent—15 times higher than that of the general population," and "about 60 percent of people with bipolar disorder have drug and/or alcohol abuse problems—the highest rate among all people with major psychiatric illnesses." According to the *Washington Post*, 1,700 children and adolescents commit suicide every year. Many suicidal young people suffer from bipolar disorder but have not been diagnosed. Yet new research may yield a better understanding of the neurobiology that can lead to bipolar disorder. New evidence suggests that genes might be responsible for transmitting bipolar disorder, and people whose parents had the condition are ten times as likely to develop the disorder.

The Society for Neuroscience writes that scientists have begun to identify irregularities in "the structure or function of the brain circuits that are involved with bipolar disorder. In addition to changes in the amygdala, researchers have found lesions in the white matter of the brains of people with bipolar disorder, particularly in areas responsible for emotional processing. Also, changes in activity in certain areas of the brain have been observed in people with bipolar disorder. Studies suggest that some of these structural and functional changes may precede the onset of symptoms and that some medications may reverse these changes—findings that may lead to ways of diagnosing and treating the disease early, before symptoms occur."

In addition to the importance of continued brain research and the development of new treatments, experts assert the need to remove the stigma that bipolar disorder still carries, a stigma that might prevent parents from seeking medical help for their children early. Gavin cites the advice of Cheryl King, the director of the Youth Depression and Suicide Prevention Program at the University of Michigan Depression Center, saying, "Both teens and adults need to understand that depression and bipolar disorder are real diseases rooted in brain chemistry and genetics, not personal failings or weaknesses. They're not the result of something they did or didn't do—and they're not something to be ashamed of. Moreover, all of these problems or conditions can be treated, with good results, if teens get professional help as early as possible."

Like diabetes or high blood pressure, bipolar disorder is a disease, and it can and should be treated. Heightened awareness among parents and teachers can help students get treatment and can help prevent suicides. Chase Edwards's parents helped enact Chase's Law in 2006, which encourages schools to teach students and staff about the dangers of depression, and Senator Smith introduced and was able to help pass the Garrett Lee Smith Memorial Act, legislation that expands suicide-prevention programs and will make counseling services on university campuses more effective.

Mental health professionals acknowledge the importance of ongoing neuroscientific developments that may lead to breakthroughs in treating bipolar disorder and other afflictions. But they point out that the first hurdle is recognizing those suffering from these disorders who may otherwise have fallen through the cracks. As Cheryl King asserts, "the biggest challenge is finding those who need treatment and getting them the help they need."

SOCIAL ISSUES
FIRSTHAND

CHAPTER 1

Living with Bipolar Disorder

Being Diagnosed with Bipolar Disorder at the Age of Fifteen

Patrick Jamieson

At age eleven the author experiences his first manic-depressive episode, but years pass before he is diagnosed correctly and can start treatment. In this selection, he chronicles his affliction from a teenage perspective and describes the highs and lows of the disease. Patrick Jamieson is associate director of the Adolescent Risk Communication Institute and the editor of the Adolescent Mental Health Initiative series of books for parents and teens.

I experienced my first manic episode at 11, just after my family moved from Maryland to Hawaii for six months. I found Hawaii dizzyingly bright, a world of billowing white clouds and blue ocean. It was there that I felt for the first time a heightened sense of energy, a reduced need for sleep, and an accelerated rush of thought and speech. No one thought anything of it. To my parents, these behaviors looked like a reasonable response to a new place filled with sun and surf. But something wasn't right, because I felt on edge and angry.

The year-round flowers and flowering plants also triggered my asthma and I started wheezing. I was taken to an asthma specialist, who sent me home with a cortisone-based inhalant—which at the time was new but now is standard treatment. Within half a day of the first breath of the inhalant, the world crashed around me. Feeling worthless, hopeless, frightened, and alone, I recoiled from those around me. Watching my retreat with alarm, my mother discontinued the inhalant and called the doctor to report that it had produced a bizarre effect. She said, "In an adult I would call Patrick's response depression." In fact, after three months of mania probably activated by the stress of the move, I was now experiencing, as an 11-year-old, a full-blown drug crash that looked just like depression—seemingly brought on by a rare reaction to the cortisone in the inhalant. Years later, a doctor told me it was probably a coincidence, but in any event it didn't last long and my mood leveled off for the rest of the time in Hawaii. Nonetheless, I remember my stay there as a disturbing and troubled time—paradise lost.

Another Move

When I was 13 years old, after a brief interlude back in Maryland, my family moved again, this time to Austin, Texas. Several months later, I started having health problems. My allergies were acting up. I picked up several sinus infections, then bronchitis. I was tired but mistakenly shrugged off my lethargy as a consequence of the bronchitis. The thought that I might be depressed never crossed the minds of my parents or any of the doctors they sought out. My reputation as an eccentric, based in the free-wheeling individualism cultivated by a Montessori education and an anti-authoritarian upbringing reinforced by my parents, explained any symptoms of mental illness. Just like my mother, who had assumed that whatever the cortisone-based inhalant was doing to me, it could not have been triggering depression in an 11-year-old. I had no idea teenagers were susceptible to depression at all, much less manic depression. Indeed, at that point, I don't think I'd ever heard manic and depression combined into a single term.

In Austin I felt like a stranger in a strange land. Texas: big refrigerators, BBQ smokehouses, and dry 104-degree Augusts. During the school year, weekends slip by too fast and Monday mornings come much too soon. My experience was this: I don't sleep well. My cat's fleas find me an appealing alternative and the air conditioner's cycle disturbs my sleep. I wake up groggy. My chest feels hollow. My heart pounds. I've slept through my alarm clock again and am late for school.

Depression Hits

In the car en route to school, I realize that something primitive has taken hold of me. My thoughts are spinning. My brain has shifted from first to fourth gear. At school, I stare transfixed in front of my locker as a crush of students shuffles around me to classes. My left hand is gripping my protractor, tangible evidence that I am enrolled in a geometry class, but I do not remember removing it from my backpack. My thoughts have moved from a trot to a full, all-out gallop and from the concrete world around me to fanciful abstraction. If my life is ordinarily a photograph, today it is like [Vincent] Van Gogh with intense color and distorted perspective.

English class is a blur. I can't focus well enough to take notes. I write silliness. "Hour Father. Lettuce prey." I obscure page after page with intersecting lines. I recall the stitching on one of my aunt's pillows, "God writes straight with crooked lines." There's nothing straight about today.

In geometry class, the representations on the board morph into artistic shapes. The two-dimensional has assumed a third dimension. The rectangle on the board is a toy box, a coffin, the transport vehicle of the starship *Enterprise*. I answer the teacher's questions absurdly. The area under the curve, I proclaim, is the negative space revealed by drawing a rectangle around the formula. The teacher has long ago written me off as a smart-ass. I create similar scenarios in later classes.

Trying to Slow My Thoughts

During the bus ride home, a classmate repeatedly pokes fun at my uncombed hair. "You're a slob," the ferret-faced preppy with wire-rim glasses says, his beady blue eyes in razor focus. Ordinarily I'd retaliate with a clever put-down, but my mind won't muster one. It is speeding on to something else. I mutter what those of delicate sensibilities would call an expletive. I relive this fragmented exchange late into the night. Instead of an incidental conversation, it becomes a full-blown morality play, or a confrontation between Wile E. Coyote and the Roadrunner—except in this scenario, the Roadrunner is uncharacteristically dragging a heavy ball and chain.

Trying to slow my thoughts tightens the leash around my neck. Have you ever tried to force yourself to be calm in bed at night when something catastrophic has happened? A relative has died. You've been in a car accident. It's impossible. My thoughts penetrate every barrier constructed to contain them. I once thought that with practice I could learn to control my thoughts when manic. That was an illusion.

In my experience, manias often forecast depression. The danger and deadliness of each are magnified when they combine to form what psychiatrists call a *mixed state*—a time when both manic and depressed symptoms surface. Years later I would recognize that my experience in Austin—the fast thoughts, lack of focus, and low energy—was a mixed state. For me, it is the most uncomfortable state to be in because it makes relating to others more difficult. My thinking is unhinged from the here and now. It's a lose-lose situation for everybody. But at the time, I had no idea what was going on. Maybe this is what it felt like to be a teenager, I thought. Maybe all of this is hormonal.

Crashing Down

Others around me were bewildered as well. During this extended period of mania followed by depression and a mixed state, my parents and I met with doctor after doctor in Austin. I was poked and probed, scanned and scrutinized. It seemed as if every bodily fluid of mine that could be extracted was tested for diseases both rare and common. After battery upon battery of tests, each doctor offered a different diagnosis. An immune system disorder, reported one. A rare form of mononucleosis, concluded another. Epstein-Barr syndrome, said a third. Allergies, proclaimed a fourth. None could produce a blood or urine test, a CT scan or MRI showing any tangible evidence for these diagnoses. They might as well have said, "We haven't got a clue."

Exhausted after months of little sleep and still less focus, I crashed out of the mixed state and into a five-month depression during which I slept up to 18 hours a day and missed more school than I attended. I started feeling well just in time to study enough to squeak past finals. As that process drew to a close, I spent increasing amounts of time with a mallet in hand, working on the timber-frame addition to our family house that my father was building outside my bedroom window.

The satisfaction of building something by hand was primitive. I sharpened my own chisels and made my own mallets. It felt good to step back and survey what I had accomplished at the end of the day, the week, and the month. Part of me was in the house. The process also felt therapeutic. The strength in my hands, arms, and shoulders seemed to carry over to my brain. Driving pegs into the wooden joints to lock them in place focused my mind.

A friend of my dad's named Jon helped with the heavy work. What I knew about him was limited to the scattered fragments of information that slipped out in conversations among adults. If he took his medication, said the whispers of adults, he was fine. When he felt well, however, he'd occasionally stop the medication and ultimately required hospitalization. His illness was called bipolar disorder.

Highs and Lows

Considered brilliant in college, he had not held a steady job since. After some sort of "breakdown," he was given lithium, a mood-stabilizing medication. I feared him at first because I didn't know what to expect from someone who had to take lithium. Around me, he seemed as normal as any other adult, married with two kids, quick, witty, and unaffected by the ultimate adult sin: He was not patronizing. At first the mystery surrounding his illness frightened me. Working on the roof of the three-story timber frame put us more than 27 feet above the ground. How safe was it to be up there with someone with a mental disorder, I wondered. The doubts evaporated quickly. He worked as hard as my dad did. They were friends. He was a good guy. What I did not know at the time was that he and his wife had seen a parallel between my highs and lows of the past academic year and Jon's own journey into bipolar disorder.

Contact with Jon was not my only early encounter with bipolar disorder. My aunt's husband, Kyle, was a charismatic, all-around guy who loved gourmet cooking, camping in the woods, whitewater rafting, canoeing, and roughing it in the wild. He also wrote music and played saxophone and rhythm guitar in a rock band. To me, he became living proof that the boring adult lives forecast by our parents—as engineers, lawyers, doctors, or professors—were not the inevitable end of growing up.

A Suicide in the Family

But there was another Kyle. The first hint of this side of him came when he failed to attend a family reunion at my grandparents'. Rumors circulated through the family. Kyle had spent months in silence in a darkened room. He had not returned home for days while engaged in marathon recording sessions with his band. This Kyle used uppers to counter his depression and downers to dampen his mania, a common practice for people with bipolar disorder. This Kyle refused my aunt's pleas to see a doctor and take prescribed medication for bipolar disorder. Faced with an ultimatum, therapy and medication or divorce, Kyle chose divorce. After that his drinking and drug use escalated. Years later, unable to lift himself from a deep depression, and unwilling to seek help, he killed himself.

I remember Kyle during a canoeing trip, when he vaulted from his canoe to help my brother and me right ours after it capsized. I remember Kyle's ludicrous story about a headless ghoul and his joking about it as he helped us build the campfire that would cook our dinner. I did not know the Kyle who ended his own life. Or perhaps I did but didn't understand.

Moving to Philadelphia

We left Austin in 1989, this time moving to Philadelphia, where I was enrolled as a sophomore in a private urban Quaker school. I was 15, and by late summer I had been transformed from someone who slept more than most to someone who didn't seem to need to sleep at all. My energy was back. That fall I had a full course load—history, English, French, and my worst subject, algebra 2—and I fell behind almost from the start. My mind was racing and my ability to focus in class came and went. The school principal called my mother. "We are concerned about Patrick," she said. "He isn't focusing, his speech is rapid, he's not making a lot of sense. I think you should take him to a doctor."

After three years in Austin, the move to Philadelphia had put me and my family in touch with a local medical teaching hospital, and with it experts who not only recognized but also studied adolescent bipolar disorder. Confronted with a 15-year-old who hadn't slept in days, could not control his thoughts, and was increasingly verbally aggressive, my primary care physician at the hospital offered two hypotheses—a thyroid malfunction or bipolar disorder. The doctors in Austin had already checked for a thyroid malfunction and found none. A blood test confirmed their conclusion, leaving a diagnosis of bipolar disorder.

When I asked if that meant that I was schizophrenic, the only label of mental illness I could readily summon, the doctor clearly ruled it out. Now I know that it is sometimes difficult to draw a line between mood or "affective" disorders like bipolar disorder and schizophrenia. Indeed, there are cases in which individuals have the symptoms of both and are diagnosed as schizoaffective.

Later, my middle-aged parents sat with me in the Youth Guidance Center, next to a middle-aged male psychiatrist with short black hair, glasses, and a graying beard. Dr. Gottstein said, "There's a good chance we're dealing with manic depression or bipolar disorder." My reaction is the same as it was when the diagnosis was first offered by my family doctor. I am stunned. Five minutes later my disbelief is still bristling. He can't be right, I think, there's nothing wrong with me but Epstein-Barr syndrome or an immune disorder. That was what the doctors in Austin had said, and I now desperately wanted to believe them. My symptoms are real. They are physical. My heart is racing. My throat is dry. This is not all in my head, I repeat to myself. I am not "mental." I am not crazy.

The Stigma of Mental Illness

If I was ill, I wanted a physical illness, not a mental illness—and I resolutely believed at the time that there was a clean distinction between the two. I wanted an illness caused by a bacterium that could be treated with an antibiotic or one produced by a splinter that could be removed by surgery. Psychiatric illness wasn't real; it was "all in your head"—the ultimate form of self-indulgent hypochondria, I thought, a cop-out for those too lazy or inept to cope with the world, a con used to bilk insurance companies and trick employers.

If it is difficult at 15 to accept a chronic illness, it is even more difficult to accept one about which much is unknown. When bipolar disorder entered my vocabulary, years after it had entered my life, I believed the stereotypes of so-called "mental illness" as much as anyone else. And one of the insidious things about stereotypes is that you think they are facts. I started trying to find information that would make sense to me and would reveal what about this condition was fact and what was fantasy. I wanted to know what this diagnosis meant for me. But the problem is that, although researchers and doctors have made great strides in understanding and treating bipolar disorder, there is still much that remains unknown about the illness, especially in adolescents, an understudied population. And so, some of what I found answered my questions, while other materials raised more concerns than they quieted.

As it was, the doctor addressing my family was a psychiatrist specializing in treatment of adolescents with bipolar disorder. I didn't want him to be right. I didn't want the stigma of a "mental illness." And I didn't want the treatment. "If this is bipolar disorder, you'll have to take lithium for the rest of your life," he said. I thought, "It's impossible! I can't even brush my teeth twice a day." I picked up fragments of what he was saying. No beer. No booze. No drugs. No dope. Weekly appointments. I felt 15 going on 40. From now on I was supposed to act grown up. I felt cheated out of being a teenager.

Hurtful Stereotypes

Although they are slowly changing, widespread Western societal stereotypes hold that being physically ill is preferable to being mentally ill, seeing a minister is better than seeing a psychotherapist, seeing a psychotherapist is better than seeing a psychiatrist, being treated as an outpatient is preferable to being treated as an inpatient, and voluntary hospitalization is preferred to involuntary hospitalization. Unfortunately, many of us deny our own conditions, even to ourselves.

Seeing a psychiatrist seemed to be an admission that I was crazy. I resented his presuming to interpret my attitudes and behavior. I resented the assumption that I was abusing alcohol and street drugs. My resentment took the form of sarcastic and sometimes savage words and a war of wills. I responded to a difficult situation by blaming my predicament on my "shrink" (as I referred to him when I was angry).

My belief that I didn't need anybody's help added to my disdain for psychiatrists. Asking for help seemed to me a sign of weakness. I was also hard on myself for not being able to solve my own problems. I felt incompetent for having to rely on a doctor and a hospital bed as tools for staying alive. Maybe this self-reliance is a macho male weakness. Like the great baseball star Joe DiMaggio, men are supposed to be able to play with pain. This thinking got me into trouble when I felt fine for an extended period, decided I had either been misdiagnosed or cured, stopped taking lithium, and relapsed.

Struggling with Treatment

Another reason that I disliked psychiatrists was that I associated them with the seemingly endless urine samples and blood tests a freshly diagnosed person encounters when attempting to get new medications balanced. I couldn't walk out of my doc's office without new prescriptions in hand. I also associated him with long lines and large bills. (Insurance that covers 100% of a so-called physical illness will often cover only half of the cost of a so-called mental one.)

As much as I resented having bipolar disorder, and having to take medication for it, I resisted even more the "talk" sessions of psychotherapy. Teenagers take privacy very seriously. These are years in which our bedrooms are off limits even to family members, years in which phone conversations with friends take on a conspiratorial tone. Into this walled-off world comes a prying adult asking very personal questions: questions about feelings and family, questions about drugs and alcohol, questions about sexual inclinations and actions, questions about sleep patterns and thoughts of suicide. The questions are troubling in part because they suggest the range of concerns that have come to preoccupy those around you.

Every query by the psychiatrist who diagnosed my condition (I had not yet awarded him the status of "my" psychiatrist) seemed like prying. I've known those who will tell anyone anything; I've never been one of them. I make friends cautiously and share confidences hesitantly. Although his attitude was nonjudgmental, the psychiatrist's questions seemed to me to be invasive. He had not earned the right to ask. I didn't trust him enough to answer.

I also didn't like having to be self-reflective on command and rebelled against the requirements of the so-called "medication management" sessions. I needed someone to blame for my anger, fear, and disbelief. True to the profile sketched by the psychology manuals, I blamed my doc.

Psychiatrists are trained to ask questions rather than to give answers. Psychiatry blends science and art to address an individual with a unique personal history. It is one of the most difficult professions around. Psychiatrists are medical school graduates with extensive residency experience. Like trauma surgeons, they keep people alive, but unlike trauma surgeons, they see their patients for weeks, months, or years. While some doctors can think of a patient as an occasional office visitor, a psychiatrist has an ongoing therapeutic relationship with a client, with the client relying on that relationship for guidance in life survival skills.

Bipolar Teenagers

Adolescents inherit more than an illness when they are diagnosed with bipolar disorder. We have to deal with frightened parents and, once diagnosed, we have to navigate a relationship with even more adults, including a psychiatrist or therapist. Teen bipolar disorder is a family problem that affects siblings and spouses, as well as parents and grandparents. To the extent that they will be called on to help us manage this disorder, they need to be brought into a relationship with the managing doctor as well.

At 16 I had a more cynical view of the client-psychiatrist relationship than I do now. I didn't think psychiatrists deserved the insurance money they were claiming for "doing nothing." I didn't think it was fair to pay my psychiatrist well over $100 every two weeks or every month to secure a prescription. Why couldn't he just phone in the prescription or give me a standing order?

Now I know that my relapse rate is much lower because I see a psychiatrist regularly. The National Institute of Mental Health says, "Studies have shown that psychosocial interventions can lead to increased mood stability, fewer hospitalizations, and improved functioning in several areas." In other words, seeing a therapist or psychiatrist is important.

What It Feels Like to Live with Bipolar Disorder

Jane Pauley, interviewed by Patrick Perry

In this selection, broadcast journalist Jane Pauley talks about her diagnosis of bipolar disorder at age 50 and how it has affected her life. She also discusses how she deals with the disease and some of the side effects of treatment. Jane Pauley is an Emmy Award–winning journalist.

For more than three decades, Jane Pauley graced our homes, a friendly face covering the events that shaped our lives. Her wholesome beauty, subtle wit, and Midwestern charm captured the hearts and admiration of millions of Americans and earned the broadcaster fame, family, and fortune beyond her wildest dreams.

While front and center on the world stage interviewing celebrities, royalty, and politicians, Pauley preferred the private life, bypassing the glare of celebrity to embrace her family, including husband, cartoonist Garry Trudeau, and their three children. In an industry that thrives on image, Pauley remained resilient, demonstrating humility and self-effacing humor rare in the primetime world of American media.

Then at age 50, Pauley was diagnosed with bipolar disorder, surprising herself, family, and colleagues alike. With courage and depth, the Emmy Award–winning journalist stepped into the public arena to share her experiences with bipolar disorder in a moving memoir, *Skywriting: A Life Out of the Blue.*

"Truth arrives in microscopic increments, and when enough has accumulated, in a moment of recognition, you

Patrick Perry, "Jane Pauley: Tackling the Stigma of Bipolar Disorder," *Saturday Evening Post*, vol. 279, no. 2, March/April 2007. © 2007 Saturday Evening Post Society. Reproduced by permission.

just know," writes Pauley in her *New York Times* bestseller. "You know because the truth fits."

With characteristic candor and warmth, Jane Pauley spoke with the *Post* about her journey of self-discovery, mental-health advocacy, and future plans.

Diagnosed at Age 50

Post: How common is a first diagnosis of bipolar disorder at the age of 50?

Jane Pauley: Not common at all, but becoming more so. I try not to confuse my experience having a mood disorder with expertise, and this is an area of disagreement among doctors, so I will tread cautiously. Bipolar disorder is known to have a strong genetic component—so it's likely that my genes predisposed me to have a mood disorder—but until I was treated with steroids for hives, it wasn't "activated" or not at a level that would have appeared outside the range of normal behavior. I had experienced low-grade depression before, but never hypomania. For the purposes of diagnosis, the fact that my first episode of hypomania was triggered by a drug prescribed for the treatment of some other illness is significant, but the practical effect was that a doctor who knew me as one of his "worried well" patients suddenly recognized symptoms of a very serious illness.

Post: Some people with bipolar suffer wild and even dangerous flights of mania and even psychoses. Were you ever manic?

Jane Pauley: Doctors have specific criteria regarding mania and hypomania. I was never at the level of mania, though I don't know how close I was. I never suffered psychosis, nor was I ever suicidal, but I was talking about a *Dateline* story I'd done in January of '01—just five months before I was hospitalized—involving a teenage girl who tried to kill herself. My doctor explained that suicide can be an impulsive gesture—and the mere fact of talking about it was a danger sign. That's why he asked me if I'd feel "more comfortable" in the hospital. I was there for three weeks.

Bipolar is considered a potentially fatal disease because the risk of suicide is so high. Friends and loved ones should know that anyone who talks about suicide—overtly or even obliquely—is in great danger.

Post: Have you had more episodes of hypomania, such as the one you wrote about in *Skywriting*? Do you expect more?

Jane Pauley: It's been five years and there's been no recurrence of hypomania, though I sometimes struggle with mild depression. Despite many wonderful antidepressants available today, doctors can't treat bipolar depression as aggressively as they would the very much more common unipolar depression because there's always the risk of triggering that rebound effect. I may never have another episode of hypomania, but I could have one and I live accordingly.

Taking Care of Herself

Post: What do you mean "live accordingly"?

Jane Pauley: I take care of myself. I take medicine the doctor prescribes; I keep him informed of changes in my moods, which sometimes means he changes my meds. I'm also learning what factors seem to affect my mood—call it "stress"— and I'm trying to learn how to modify those stressors. I've only recently learned that cognitive behavior therapy can be beneficial for people with bipolar disorder. Knowing it was a biologically based disease, I didn't think psychotherapy had much to offer, but learning how to navigate life's difficulties more productively can make life less stressful. That makes sense to me.

What doesn't make sense is why compliance is so low. I meet a lot of people who say, "I have what you have" or who have a loved one who suffers with bipolar disorder, and I always ask if they're taking care of themselves. "Not really" is the most common answer.

Post: Why do you think that is?

Jane Pauley: Bipolar disorder is a baffling disease. While science is learning more about the brain every day—with technology that scientists would not have believed possible until recently—not enough is known about the causes of bipolar. And while there are dozens of pharmacological alternatives, finding the right one or the right combinations is sometimes a trial-and-error process. It may take time to get it right. And there may be side effects that undermine compliance.

Post: Have you suffered side effects?

Jane Pauley: Lithium is associated with weight gain—so yes to that. And sometimes tremors: shaky hands and wobbly knees were unnerving at first. I remember struggling to get a spoonful of soup in my mouth at first, and the time I was offered tongs to grasp a sugar cube and flipped it six feet across the room! But one big advantage of being able to talk publicly about having a mood disorder is that I can explain why and laugh about it!

Post: Have you experienced the stigma against mental illness?

Jane Pauley: Not that I have been aware of, but I don't expect it, so I'm not on the lookout. If I was terribly sensitive to stigma, I'm sure it would be easy to spot every day.

Not Sick Enough to Be Hospitalized

Anonymous

A highly functioning woman with bipolar disorder and border-line personality disorder, the author decides to admit herself to an impatient program when her self-injury runs out of control. She details how being well-spoken and calm cause her to be rejected from admission to the program. The author is pursuing a doctoral degree in psychology.

Within my most powerful episodes of depression, I would awake each morning, shower, apply makeup, and attempt to create a fabulous outfit. My worst appearance offense during these periods would be to go out in public in a pair of bright pink sweatpants with a hooded sweatshirt—but the makeup and hair were always done.

I would do what was required of me—attend work, my internship, and classes. At school, I focused on the blackboard through tears, isolating myself from my classmates by default. None of them, I would learn later on, wanted to talk with me because my facade was intimidating. They said I looked like I didn't want to be bothered.

Looking out of a Snow Globe

When I did not have to fulfill obligations within these episodes, I would literally spend all of my time sleeping, or lying on the couch. I described my life as that of looking out of a snow globe—my world had ceased movement and I watched everyone around me carry on at normal pace. My chest constantly felt as though I was wearing a weight upon it—yet the contents of my chest were that of nothing—hollow and empty inside. I would lay on the sofa, extremely thirsty for extended periods of time, too depressed to walk into the kitchen and pour myself a drink.

I am 27 years old. In May, I received my master's degree in clinical and counseling psychology. I completed the semester with a 3.94 GPA and obtained admission as a second year student into the doctoral program at Chestnut Hill College where I will pursue my Psy.D. I have accepted a job as a psychotherapist at an outpatient mental health clinic. I am married and my husband and I own a house in South Philadelphia. We have three parrots, of which I am . . . caretaker. I write and publish poetry, and enjoy going to poetry workshops, giving readings, and creating abstract art.

In addition to the above, I also have diagnoses of bipolar disorder NOS [Not Otherwise Specified], borderline personality disorder, and generalized anxiety disorder. I am a chronic self-injurer and I cut myself on a daily basis. I have intense mood swings, bouts of severe depression, various impulsive and self-destructive behaviors, mixed episodes, relentless agitation and anxiety, and recurrent suicidal ideation.

Seeking Help

On April 29th, 2008, at the strong urging of my psychiatrist and therapist, I packed my belongings and my husband drove me to Friends Hospital in Philadelphia. The main reason for seeking an inpatient stay was my self-injury, which had become completely out of control. I have been self-injuring for nine years, but this was by far the worst it had ever gotten. Despite the work I had been doing with my therapist, it seemed as though the only way for me to break the cycle of self-injury would be to place myself in a controlled environment, in which the means to self-injure would be absent.

In addition to the cutting, I was also engaging in various [other] self-destructive behaviors, which served as ways to almost cross the line of my suicidal ideation. These behaviors included putting a large number of tranquilizers into my mouth and then spitting them out, cutting my wrists, but not enough to do any serious damage, and engaging in reckless driving. There are nights in which I cut, but I have no recollection of the action. I wake up the following morning and the bandages are there—I struggle to recall the behavior, but it is as though it never happened. There are also times in which my mood reaches a manic irritability, in which the razor swipes down and hits like a hammer. I feel nothing. These are the times in which I have lost the most control and end up cutting deeper than I had intended.

When I arrived at the hospital for my intake [admission], I was dressed well, but casually. My hair was styled and I was wearing makeup, as I always do. When I interviewed with the psychiatrist, I told him my diagnoses. He asked what I did for a living and when I told him about my career and level of education, he looked surprised, as though I was the first doctoral student to ever set foot in a psychiatric hospital. I used terms like "depersonalization" and "psychodynamic"—not to be obnoxious, but because that is the language I know and the best way, I feel, to deliver information to a psychiatrist. I gave insight into my cutting behavior, splitting it into three groups—the need to relieve agitation, the addiction, and the piece of my identity that I am too fearful to give up. I spoke to him about the difference between my hypomanic episodes fueling creativity in my poetry versus the natural creativity itself. I told him how I felt I could benefit from the structured environment of the hospital in addition to the intensive groups. I explained that in therapy, I explore the underlying meanings of my behaviors, but at this time it was too out of control and I needed a different type of intervention.

I also told him about the mouthful of tranquilizers, the erratic driving, suicidal ideation, and the agitated manias. I showed him my scars and told him that the last time I cut was about 10 minutes before I left to go to the hospital. I expressed my fear of cutting deeper than I meant to, or in a place where I shouldn't have cut at all.

It was then that the doctor told me that he didn't believe that I would benefit from inpatient hospitalization. He stated that the criteria they use in the Crisis Response Center is to think about whether if they sent an individual home after the evaluation, would he or she die? He didn't think I would die. He said that I wasn't in any immediate danger and that obviously, my daily living skills were excellent. He mentioned that the other individuals on the unit were "sick." He then offered to me and my husband to stay around for a few more minutes while he consulted with another psychiatrist on staff.

I recall the days prior to going to the hospital when I was supposed to be packing and getting emotionally prepared for this. My husband calls me on his way home from work.

"What are you doing?" he asked me.

"Oh, I have a 4:45 appointment to get my eyebrows waxed. I'll be home a little bit after 5:00."

(Who the hell worries about what their eyebrows look like two days before they go into a psychiatric hospital?)

"But that's part of what makes you, you," my husband tells me. He's so right.

Now I will make a shift to one night before the hospitalization. My husband calls me from the train. He's on his way home from New York.

"What are you doing?"

"Oh, just a little pre–mental hospitalization shopping. You're never going to believe what I got! I found these socks with a sparkly, insane looking cat on them, holding a chainsaw—then they say on them—don't make the crazy girl mad! How perfect is that?"

And so my husband and I sat in the waiting room of the Crisis Response Center—me with my perfectly shaped eyebrows, bag packed with my new socks that I was way too excited to wear, all of my beauty products, and my books. . . .

The psychiatrist eventually returned and invited me and my husband into a small office, where we met another doctor. This doctor expressed his agreement with the evaluating psychiatrist—that I was not appropriate for inpatient hospitalization.

"Do you ever fear that the cutting will become dangerous?" he asked me.

"Doctor," I answered him. "I believe it already has. But if you are speaking about a matter of life and death, all I can tell you is that sometimes I don't know how deep I'm cutting, or where the cut is going to land. Sometimes I cut my wrist, but not deep enough to do any serious damage. What if, in one of my impulsive, out-of-my-mind times, it lands there really deep?"

"Yes," he answered. "I would be concerned about that, too."

"Failing" My Hospital Interview

The doctor then offered me the recommendation of partial hospitalization. I asked him, already knowing the answer, if he could please explain to me, the type of individuals that would show up in the partial-hospital program.

"Typically low-functioning clients," he responded.

"Individuals who require assistance with their daily living skills?"

Both psychiatrists confirmed this. One stated that he only suggested it because he didn't want to prejudice me against any treatment. He added that he hoped I had a good relationship with my therapist, and would be able to increase my sessions each week. I told him it was great—a great non-insurance relationship. He said, "Oh. Well, at least it's a great relationship." I left the hospital that night angry and defeated—and with no more intensive treatment than I had gone in with.

Once I left the hospital, I left a message for my therapist in a torrent of animated, angry words. I stated to him, "I got past a doctoral school interview, a therapist job interview, but I can't get past a psychiatric hospital interview?"

That irony has a powerful truth to it. Those first two interviews had required me to dress well and speak intellectually and openly. Apparently I had done the same thing with the psychiatrist at the hospital, only the content was different—I was telling him of my pain, self-destructive behaviors, and suicidal ideation. I was also engaging the doctor in some light debate, based on a question he had asked me in regards to hypomanic mood and creativity. I couldn't get past a psychiatric hospital interview because I was acting too much like myself.

I came to this conclusion a couple of days later as I sat with the women in my borderline personality disorder support group. I recounted the story of my failed hospitalization and a couple of the women stated that perhaps I had been too intellectual and not enough emotional. As we talked about the possibility of trying admission into another hospital, the women suggested that I "leave the adult at home" next time I go for an evaluation.

High Functioning but Mentally Ill

I didn't understand why I would have to leave an entire compartment of my personality at home, or put it to sleep. This was my true self. I felt it unfair that if I showed up as my true self, with all of the pain and need for help underneath, that I wouldn't be perceived as "sick" enough to be in the hospital.

Obviously a stigma exists . . . within all aspects of mental illness. However, I have always been aware of a separate stigma for those who are mentally ill, but functioning at a high level. When I say functioning at a high level, I am referring to a variety of factors in any combination: these individuals may have graduate degrees or are actively involved in attending school, hold professional jobs, [be] of a middle to high economic status, and have optimal daily living skills (in regards to hygiene, dressing, grooming). They may present well, speak well, and not appear "sick" to even the most seasoned therapist or psychiatrist.

My saddened affect has been perceived by my coworkers and school peers as though I am stuck-up, unapproachable, or isolative. At home, I was writing research papers through tears and cutting myself, sometimes up to 20 times each night. However, it was winter so I was able to easily cover my cuts and I was just viewed as being just a bit unfriendly—certainly not ill.

One summer semester I was taking a psychopharmacology class. We were learning about the mood stabilizers and antipsychotics. My professor made a passing comment pertaining to how he was sure that "no one in the class had a serious diagnosis such as bipolar disorder or schizophrenia," which, in effect, meant that nobody in the class could be taking such medications. Little did he know, one of the few individuals who got an A in that class carried three mental health diagnoses and had been on 15 different psychiatric medications by that time.

My husband recently told me he "fell victim" to not [believing] that I was, in fact, ill, and that I have been [well] for the entire time he has known me and even before that. He stated that he thought that since I work hard, gave therapy to patients at my internship, maintained a [GPA near 4.0], was accepted into doctoral school, and care deeply about my appearance, that it couldn't be "real." He revealed to me that he is just now beginning to understand the pain and severity of what I go through. It is an unbelievable, yet powerful symbol of the misunderstanding of mental illness—that someone I have known for seven years and lived with for six, could not conceive of the reality of my suffering.

This also holds true for my parents, who were shocked when I told them about my decision to attempt inpatient hospitalization: "But you were doing so well—I mean, you look great, you are doing—wait, how is it that you can be ill and yet know so much about psychology?"

I had to explain to them how there was no connection between having an illness and working in the field of psychology. I had to explain to them that just because I was able to meet occupational and educational demands, an illness can still exist.

If my husband could not see it, how could I expect a psychiatrist to recognize it during a ten minute intake? No, I did not show up to the intake falling apart. I wasn't crying, screaming, hallucinating, or even with a particularly depressed affect. However, I did show up with a well-spoken appeal for help, in an effort to take control over my self-destructive nature. I presented as a pink-shoe-wearing therapist, [a] doctoral student with insights and purse to match. Underneath, I am a frightened, exhausted, confused, destructive, impulsive, sometimes little girl, with forceful and dangerous mood swings.

I truly believe that if I had shown up that night with the exact same story, but different presentation, I would have gotten the help that I needed. It leaves me with this question: Where do I, and other individuals like me, exist on the treatment spectrum? Yes, we have our private psychiatrists and therapists—but what happens when we need a greater level of care? My personal experience exemplifies a struggle in simply trying to get someone to recognize that I am ill enough to need intensive treatment.

The Urge to Self-Injure

As I write this, I would like to say that I am fighting the urge to self-injure, but that would be a false claim. It is an impulse that is much bigger than my resolve and has not ceased or slowed down since my unsuccessful intake at the hospital. I was offered another try by my psychiatrist and therapist, to be admitted into the hospital with intense support from them in order to gain admission. I declined because of the unpleasant, yet realistic disconnection in being ill, but highly functioning. This means that I have an obligation and a vast drive to begin my new job as a therapist. This also means that at the same time, I will be dealing with all of the symptoms that I have previously described. For the most part, I have always managed to keep my illness from interfering with my professional and academic life. I suppose this is why it is difficult for some to realize that there is an illness at all. However, I never forget because every day is a struggle of mood swings, impulses, and chronic emptiness.

I would like to think that at this moment, I should have been in a safer place than I am now. Or perhaps by this time, I would have been discharged and would have had some time to break the destructive cycle I am in. Maybe I would have benefited from the short-term skill-based therapy that I am not presently used to. Conceivably, the psychiatrists at the hospital may have adjusted my medications a bit in order to better stabilize my mood in a safe environment.

Unfortunately, none of these things could materialize. Frankly, I will probably continue to self-injure until I either do something incredibly dangerous (which I am afraid of), or until I am just ready to stop. I will continue to see my psychiatrist and will deal with medication adjustments and side effects while working and going to school.

Nine years ago, when I lived in New York, I was voluntarily hospitalized for very similar reasons. It was somewhat of a traumatic experience. All of these years [since], I lived in fear of the hospital, thinking it was only a place that could devastate one further. At the age of 27, I finally conjured up enough courage to reach out for the help that I needed, despite my intense fear of the hospital. I was denied. I was denied from the hospital because I did not "appear" sick enough.

A Pregnant Woman Lives Through Postpartum Psychosis

Bipolar Chica

Diagnosed with bipolar disorder, the writer finds that pregnancy threatens to push her over the edge. She recounts how, after giving birth, the combination of sleep deprivation and her disorder cause her to have thoughts of harming her child. She encourages other pregnant women with bipolar disorder to seek help with child care to treat their disorder as soon as possible after giving birth.

Everyone's heard a postpartum story, even if only on the news. We all the know the story of Andrea Yates, who drowned her five children . . . a short time after giving birth to her last child. Andrea believed that her children were to perish in the fires of hell because she was not righteous. Andrea was in psychiatric care for depression for over two years before this incident.

One or two in a thousand women end up in postpartum psychosis and I happened to be one of them. I gave birth to a healthy baby girl in April of 2007. It had been a difficult pregnancy. Two months into my pregnancy I learned I had Bipolar Disorder. I was relieved to know that there had been something wrong with me all this time. I thought that I could finally get some help. I wasn't given any mood stabilizers while I was pregnant. They weren't sure what the medications would do to the fetus I was carrying. I spent the entire ten months in a state of anxiety and depression that made me claw at my skin. I didn't know what was happening to me. It was an awful time in my life.

Bipolar Chica, "I Lived Through Postpartum Psychosis," Bipolarchica.com, June 2008. Reproduced by permission.

Postpartum Depression

A little over a month after giving birth, I went into postpartum depression. I knew I was in postpartum and I even went to the doctor. I was put on Lamictal and Zyprexa. I just don't think there was enough time for it to work. My mood fluctuated from mania to anger to anxiety to depression. I remember obsessively cleaning my house in the middle of the night. I began thinking that I was a horrible mother. I dreamt of how I would kill myself. And then one day I began having horrible thoughts. I became resentful of my baby. The baby wouldn't sleep long enough. The baby cried too much and I felt overwhelmed. I was alone all day with the baby and a three year old. My husband commuted to his work over an hour away.

I became a person I didn't recognize. I shouted for my baby to shut up and had an urge to shake her. I managed to resist the urge. The next day the urge was worse. I called my doctor and left her a message because I knew I needed help. I sobbed and laid my baby back in her bassinet. I couldn't stop crying. I called my husband to come home immediately. I called my doctor again and left another message. I knew I was in a bad way and the realization of it calmed me a little. After rocking my baby, I fell asleep holding her. She was finally quiet and I was glad. I woke up, opened my eyes, and saw two androids/aliens standing at the end of my chair and they were holding out their arms to take the baby away from me. I clutched my baby closer, blinked, and they were gone. I got up and put the baby in the bassinet and sobbed uncontrollably while I waited for my husband to get home. I felt so ashamed.

I finally got a call from my doctor around 5:30 that evening. I told her what was going on. At first, she wanted to give me an antidepressant added to the Lamictal and Zyprexa that I was already taking. I argued that would send me into mania and I didn't want that. To complicate things further I told her about the urge to shake the baby and the androids.

That sent her over the edge and she told me to go to the mental hospital. I argued with her and cried. She asked to speak to my husband and somehow she convinced him of my need to go. After a little coaxing from him, I finally agreed to go.

The Mental Hospital

We drove an hour to reach the mental pokey. The building was old and only had 5 floors. I had trepidation just looking at it. We entered and immediately were met with guards who wanted to ransack our bags and put paper bracelets on our wrists. After a short discussion on whether or not cell phones were allowed we were told to go to the fifth floor for assessment. Up we went. The elevator door chimed and we got out and found a lady who asked me to fill out paperwork. It seemed very surreal. The hospital looked normal and sounded normal and so did the people who filled the waiting room. Was I in the right place?

I saw a nurse who took my vitals and asked me what meds I was on. Then I saw a social worker who asked me a million questions about why I was there. After I told him that I didn't want to share my information with him since he could get my kids taken away from him he assured me that I wouldn't get my kids taken away. I told him my story and he wasn't shocked. I'm sure it was old hat to him, but to me it was terrifying. I saw the doctor next who wanted to admit me for 2–3 days. He said it was as much for my sake as it was for the children's.

I went to the waiting room for a nurse to come get me. I had a dinner while I waited. My husband asked me if I was sure that I wanted to stay. He was sad that he was going to be away from me. He teared up even. He told me that he could stay home with me for a few days to see if that helped so I wouldn't have to stay there. The nurse came to get me and so I could begin signing myself away on paperwork. I didn't want to sign away my freedom so easily so I asked for a Power of Attorney form. While she went to get it I began reading all the small print. The part on the amount of money this would cost, even with insurance, made me pause. We couldn't afford $1500 even if we were put on a payment plan. I decided to leave. After I got home I wasn't so sure that I did the right thing.

Feeling Like a Monster

I felt like I had been living in a horror movie. How could I, even for a second, have thought about harming my precious little baby? What chemical imbalance made me this monster? I forced myself to start having more positive thoughts and I let go of my pride and asked for help from my in-laws. I spent a week with them and the kids and I spent another week with my father and my husband. They helped me so much during that time. I shudder to think what would've been my fate without them. Would I have ended up like Andrea Yates? Would my children have ended up like her children?

If you or someone you know has bipolar disorder and gives birth, please tell them about my story. It is more likely that they will have postpartum psychosis. The mother should never spend most of her time alone with an infant because this could lead to severe sleep deprivation. Constant contact with a psychiatrist or therapist during the first six weeks after a child's birth is highly recommended. If there's a choice between meds and breast feeding to be made, please choose the medications. The sooner treatment is sought in postpartum, the better. This [condition] can be controlled with medication. There are options out there. There is help.

My little baby is now fourteen months. She said "Mama" last week and "Dada" just yesterday. I am so very thankful that she is here. When I think back upon what could've happened, I still get teary eyed. She's so beautiful and she lights up a room. I will always be thankful to the people who helped me get through that time in my life. We are never alone in our walk through life, not when we truly need it.

Coming to Terms with Being Bipolar

Anna Pearce and Matt Scanlon

In this selection, actress Patty Duke discusses her childhood struggles with anxiety and depression that became full bipolar disorder in her teenage years. She recounts some of the manic episodes and misdiagnoses that occurred during her acting career and how a correct diagnosis and treatment with lithium finally helped her to manage her disease. Patty Duke was born Anna Marie Duke and has had a long, successful acting career, beginning when she was just a child.

If [Charles] Dickens had written a book about Hollywood, he could not have penned a childhood more desperate yet inspirational than Patty Duke's. Born Anna Marie Duke in 1948, Patty was systematically alienated and virtually kidnapped from her troubled mother and alcoholic father by talent managers Ethel and John Ross at an age when most children are learning their ABC's. In the hands of the Rosses, she endured unabated abuse for more than a decade. Her startling acting talent was at once a key to escaping the sorrow of her life and a doorway to a mental affliction that very nearly took her life.

When she was 7, Duke was already smiling in commercials and small television parts. Next, her young career led her to Broadway and later to a role as Helen Keller in a stage version of *The Miracle Worker*. She starred in a screen adaptation of the play, which garnered a frenzy of praise and an Oscar, and she was later offered her own TV series. *The Patty Duke Show*'s hugely popular three-year run in the mid-1960s clinched her

Anna Pearce and Matt Scanlon, "Through a Lens, Darkly," *Psychology Today*, vol. 35, no. 4, July–August 2002, pp. 66–68. Copyright © 1991–2007 Sussex Publishers LLC. Reproduced by permission.

status as a teen icon. Yet Anna was never able to find joy in her success. She would endure a long struggle with manic depression and medicinal misdiagnoses before she would find the girl she was forced to pronounce "dead" and learn to live her life without fear. In a *Psychology Today* exclusive, she discusses some key moments on the path to her well-being.

Childhood Struggles

I was 9 years old and sitting alone in the back of a cab as it rumbled over New York City's 59th Street bridge. No one was able to come with me that day. So there I was, a tough little actor handling a Manhattan audition on my own. I watched the East River roll into the Atlantic, then I noticed the driver who was watching me curiously. My feet began tapping and then shaking, and slowly, my chest grew tight and I couldn't get enough air in my lungs. I tried to disguise the little screams I made as throat clearings, but the noises began to rattle the driver. I knew a panic attack was coming on, but I had to hold on, get to the studio and get through the audition. Still, if I kept riding in that car I was certain that I was going to die. The black water was just a few hundred feet below.

"Stop!" I screamed at him. "Stop right here, please! I have to get out!"

"Young miss, I can't stop here."

"Stop!"

I must have looked like I meant it, because we squealed to a halt in the middle of traffic. I got out and began to run, then sprint. I ran the entire length of the bridge and kept going. Death would never catch me as long as my small legs kept propelling me forward. The anxiety, mania and depression that would mark much of my life was just beginning.

Ethel Ross, my agent and substitute parent, was combing my hair one day a few years earlier, wrestling furiously with the tangles and knots that formed on my head, when she said, "Anna Marie Duke, Anna Marie. It's not perky enough." She forced her way through a particularly tough hair bramble as I winced. "OK, we've finally decided," she declared "You are gonna change your name. Anna Marie is dead. You are Patty, now."

I was Patty Duke. Motherless, fatherless, scared to death and determined to act my way out of sadness but feeling as if I was already going crazy.

Although I don't think that my bipolar disorder fully manifested itself until I was about 17, I had struggles with anxiety and depression throughout my childhood. I have to wonder, as I look at old films of mine when I was a child, where I got that shimmering, supernatural energy. It seems to me that it came from three things: mania, fear of the Rosses and talent. Somehow I had to, as a child of 8, understand why my mother, to whom I was attached at the hip, had abandoned me. It may be that part of her knew that the Rosses could better manage my career. And maybe it was partly due to her depression. All I knew was that I barely saw my mother and that Ethel discouraged even the smallest contact with her.

Because I wasn't able to express anger or hurt or rage, I began a very unhappy and decades' long pursuit of denial just to impress those around me. It's odd and thoroughly displeasing to recall, but I do think that my unnatural vivacity in my very early movies was largely because acting was the only outlet I had for exorcising my emotions.

Episodes of Mania and Depression

While working on *The Miracle Worker* play, the movie and later, *The Patty Duke Show*, I began to experience the first episodes of mania and depression. Of course, a specific diagnosis was unavailable then, so each condition was either ignored, scoffed at by the Rosses or medicated by them with impressive amounts of stelazine or thorazine. The Rosses seemed to have an inexhaustible amount of drugs. When I needed to be ratcheted down during a crying spell at night, the drugs were always there. I understand now, of course, that both stelazine and thorazine are antipsychotic medications, worthless in the treatment of manic depression. In fact, they may well have made my condition worse. I slept long, but never well.

The premise of *The Patty Duke Show* was a direct result of a few days spent with TV writer Sydney Sheldon, and if I'd had enough wit at the time, the irony would have deafened me. ABC wanted to strike while my stardom iron was still hot and produce a series, but neither I nor Sidney nor the network had an idea as to where to begin. After several talks, Sidney, jokingly but with some conviction, pronounced me "schizoid." He then produced a screenplay in which I was to play two identical 16-year-old cousins: the plucky, irascible, chatty Patty and the quiet, cerebral and thoroughly understated Cathy. The uniqueness of watching me act out a modestly bipolar pair of cousins when I was just beginning to suspect the nature of the actual illness swimming below the surface must have given the show some zing, because it became a huge hit. It ran for 104 episodes, though the Rosses forbade me from watching a single one . . . lest I develop a big head.

The disease came over me slowly in my late teens, so slowly and with such duration of both manic and depressive states that it was tough to tell just how sick I had become. It was all the more difficult because I would very often feel just fine and rejoice in the success I had. I was made to feel coveted and invulnerable, despite the fact that I came home to the Rosses who treated me as a thankless, bumbling ingrate. By 1965, I was able to see the awfulness of their home and their lives, so I found the courage to say that I would never set foot in their house again. I moved to Los Angeles to shoot the third season of *The Patty Duke Show* and started my tenth year as an actor. I was 18.

There were successes thereafter, and plenty of failures, but my struggle always concerned my bipolar disorder more than the eccentricities and paper-thinness of Hollywood or the challenges of family life. I married, I divorced, I drank and I smoked like a munitions factory. I cried for days at a time in my twenties and worried the hell out of those close to me.

One day during that period, I got into my car and thought I heard on the radio that there had been a coup at the White House. I learned the number of intruders and the plan they had concocted to overthrow the government. Then I became convinced that the only person who could address and remedy this amazing situation was me.

I raced home, threw a bag together, called the airport, booked a red-eye flight to Washington and arrived at Dulles Airport just before dawn. When I got to my hotel, I immediately called the White House and actually spoke to people there. All things considered, they were wonderful. They said that I had misinterpreted the events of the day, and as I spoke to them I began to feel the mania drain from me. In a very, very real sense I awoke in a strange hotel room, 3,000 miles from home and had to pick up the pieces of my manic episode. That was just one of the dangers of the disease: to wake up and be somewhere else, with someone else, even married to someone else.

When I was manic, I owned the world. There were no consequences for any of my actions. It was normal to be out all night, waking up hours later next to someone I didn't know. While it was thrilling, there were overtones of guilt (I'm Irish, of course). I thought I knew what you were going to say before you said it. I was privy to flights of fancy that the rest of the world could scarcely contemplate.

Through all of the hospitalizations (and there were several) and the years of psychoanalysis, the term manic-depressive was never used to describe me. I have to take some of the credit (or blame) for that, because I was also a master at disguising and defending my emotions. When the bipolar swung to the sad side, I was accomplished at using lengthy spells of crying to hide what was bothering me. At the psychiatrist's office, I would sob for the entire 45 minutes. In retrospect, I used it as a disguise; it kept me from discussing the loss of my childhood and the terror of each new day.

I'd cry, it seemed, for years at a time. When you do this, you don't need to say or do anything else. A therapist would simply ask, "What are you feeling?" and I'd sit and cry for 45 minutes. But I would work out excuses to miss therapy, and some of these plans took days to concoct.

The Diagnosis That Saved Her Life

In 1982 I was filming an episode of the series *It Takes Two* when my voice gave out. I was taken to a doctor who gave me a shot of cortisone, which is a fairly innocuous treatment for most people, with the exception of manic-depressives. For the next week I battled an all too familiar anxiety. I could barely get out of the bathroom. My voice cadence changed, my speech began to race, and I was virtually incomprehensible to everyone around me. I literally vibrated.

I lost a noticeable amount of weight in just a few days and was finally sent to a psychiatrist, who told me he suspected I had manic-depressive disorder and that he would like to give me lithium. I was amazed that someone actually had a different solution that might help.

Lithium saved my life. After just a few weeks on the drug, death-based thoughts were no longer the first I had when I got up and the last when I went to bed. The nightmare that had spanned 30 years was over. I'm not a Stepford wife; I still feel the exultation and sadness that any person feels, I'm just not required to feel them 10 times as long or as intensively as I used to.

I still struggle with depression, but it is different and not as dramatic. I don't take to my bed and cry for days. The world, and myself, just gets very quiet. That's the time for therapy, counseling or a job.

My only regret is the time lost in a haze of despair. Almost at the exact moment I began to feel better, I entered a demographic in show business whose members are hard-pressed for work. I've never felt more capable of performing well, of taking on roles with every ounce of enthusiasm and ability, only to find that there are precious few roles for a woman in her fifties. The joke in our house was "I finally got my head together and my ass fell off."

I can be, and often am, sad, but not bitter. When my daughter died in an automobile accident in 2001, I was forced to take a long look at bitterness and regret and sadness. The process of missing her and rebuilding myself will continue for years, but I know that the children, friends and love I have will plant seeds and patch holes I didn't even know were there. I worry more about the people who struggle with sadness alone, and there are millions of them.

Just the other day I was walking through a parking lot and heard a woman yell, "Is that Patty?" I saw how she moved, how her eyes danced and I listened to her frenzied vocabulary. She was bipolar. I spoke with this woman for a few minutes, and she told me of her struggles with the disease, that she was having a tough time of it lately but that she appreciated my help in championing manic depression. The implication was that if I could make it, she could. Damn straight.

In the Grip of Ups and Downs

Ryan Christman

This essay takes the reader into the mind and the desperation of a young man with bipolar disorder. He paints a vivid picture of his mind's restlessness and self-destructiveness. Ryan Christman is a creative writing student who has dedicated himself to raising awareness of bipolar disorder.

Around the corner from the Logan Square bus stop I pry open the massive window of my third-story apartment in a dilapidated 19th-century graystone that reeks of squalor[,] and before I write an email I wonder about the dimensions of my cell so I grab my 12-inch wooden ruler and move it along the walls[,] pushing aside furniture[,] and after finding it to be 10 feet square I am curious how many quarter inches that would be and then how many millimeters[,] so while I calculate I lie down on my back on the flea-ridden, plaid futon that came with the furnished apartment [and] that every morning produces fresh bites somewhere on my body[,] and I put my feet up on the wall and kick them to the rhythm of the music I have just begun to compose in my mind.

But I can't sit still so I jump up from the futon to shadow box and speculate about whether I could have been an Olympic boxer while every so often switching to various calisthenics I learned as a cadet in Air Force ROTC at Notre Dame and stopping periodically to re-organize my book collection by author then subject then color then size before having an epiphany that the absolute chaos of bipolar disorder actually paradoxically introduces a strange sense of peace into one's life because one learns to let go and accept the confusion of

Ryan Christman, "The Fierce Wind Is Wearing Me Down," *Notre Dame Magazine*, Winter 2007–2008. Reproduced by permission.

the world instead of trying to change things[,] so realizing the error of my ways and embracing chaos[,] I knock the books off the shelf and change my shirt to pure blue to reflect the deep blue calm of resignation.

A Long Way Home

Sadness sets in and my throat chokes up and tears begin to well and I sing nearly shouting: *It's a long way home, a long way from here, but surprise, blue eyes, you're already here* . . . and my neighbor pounds on the paper-thin walls and curses me but I can't help singing this song about how home is a not a physical place but a state of mind[,] or something inside ourselves[,] and I can be at home anywhere if I focus hard enough and master my demons quelling my turbulent emotions.

Contemplating the meaning of home forces me to think of my years at Notre Dame so I dig through the mountains of clothes[,] and late bills[,] and debt-consolidation offers[,] and contribution forms for charities I have volunteered to donate to[,] and obscure magazines I have ordered[,] and notifications that my car is being repossessed[,] and writing and drawings that I have strewn across the floor until I find my latest copy of *Notre Dame Magazine* and my student loan bill[,] the two of which I stick together with scotch tape and affix . . . to the wall[,] using a gold 2nd lieutenant's bar as a push pin into the aging drywall to remind myself of the great costs I paid in order to have a top education.

I begin to cry and I'm hungry now as I begin to think about my current situation and that I haven't eaten in two days so I retreat to my financial reserves which are pennies[,] mostly[,] stacked in little towers on the windowsill but I don't have enough money even for a Coke and barely enough for some cheap candy and I remember how much weight I need to lose so I start doing jumping jacks[,] stopping only once to take off my matching green sock and blue sock because[,] the more I think about it[,] the green sock should be on my right foot since green represents nature and balance and[,] after testing my balance[,] I am much more balanced on the right foot.

Using this manner of thinking I think to myself, "the right is right, right? If two wrongs don't make a right, then what do three wrongs make?" These questions amuse and amaze me so I laugh in delight and I go to the most profound book I know: *The Symbiotic Man* by Joel De Rosnay who is a French scientist who writes about the evolution of humankind and I think that this is a man who would know the answer to my questions so I open the book and amazingly within 30 seconds of searching I find direct references to the lyrics I had just composed in my mind.

I really need a Coke, so I throw on my Notre Dame flip flops that match my blue sock but not the green one so I trade the green sock for a gold sock and grab my keys and head out the door.

Living in a Halfway House

I step out into the stale-smelling pink and silver painted hallway and hear that Crazy Indian Chief guy shouting war calls again and see the landlady pounding on his door again[,] threatening to call the police[,] and [I] start down the stairs thinking to myself that Chicago is such a nice town if you have money but oppressive if you don't and I begin to cry again when I reach the second floor and I reflect on the fact that two is an oppositionary number which perfectly matches the natural conflict within my mind and I continue on to the first floor which has a nicer community shower than my floor but I know that ugly junkie couple used to have sex in there keeping me up at night when I lived on the first floor which is so gross I try not to picture it and I remember that one of the thieves of the building lives on this floor as well . . . oh, crap! Did I lock my door? How did I ever end up in a halfway house?

I re-climb the steps and lock my door and descend again until I find my way down on the street and everything begins to overwhelm me. Everyone is looking at me as if they know all about me and my situation and they look like they are laughing. No, they most definitely are laughing. The traffic is so loud. The noise is overwhelming. The crowds. The idea of riding the bus now that my car is gone. The thought of the crowded grocery store. Suddenly I'm tired. I can hear the overwhelming sound of the leaves cutting through the No-vember air and scraping against the sidewalk. The fierce wind is wearing me down. *It's not like the wind at my mom's house in Ohio. Everything is peaceful there. I miss home.*

I try to shut out the calls of the late-night transvestite prostitutes and make my way through the brisk evening to the ATM machine. I sift through my credit cards, one by one, and slip them into the machine. One after another, they are denied.

I need answers and my mind desperately races ahead in search of them. Maybe I can beg for two dollars for a Coke[,] or maybe the guy at the all-night burger shop will give me one on credit since I've been a good customer or maybe my landlady will float me another 10 bucks and then I could get dinner too at the all-night Mexican restaurant on the corner and maybe they have karaoke again tonight and maybe they would let me sing my song a cappella and maybe there's an agent in the restaurant and I could be discovered and have a recording contract but it doesn't matter because my landlady is probably back in bed by now.

Going Home

My cell phone was shut off weeks ago but suddenly I remember the $5 calling card they gave me over the weekend in the hospital [and] that I put in my wallet so I run over to the pay phone to make a call but the numbers get all jumbled up in my mind and I can't dial the right digits for some time before I finally get through.

The phone rings for a long time, and then finally my mom answers.

"Ryan? Do you know what time it is?"

"Mom, they forced me to resign from work today when I got back from the hospital after I told them that I'm bipolar and I don't know if they can do that but I went to Equal Opportunity Commission and they told me I don't have enough evidence to make a case . . ."

"Ryan. Ryan, slow down. I want you to take a deep breath, I can hardly understand you."

I'm crying now, "I need to come home. Can I come home?"

SOCIAL ISSUES
FIRSTHAND

CHAPTER 2

Coping with a Loved One's Bipolar Disorder

My Dad's Disorder

Becky Aarons

The author, a seventh-grade girl, talks about her father's bipolar personality disorder. She describes how frightening his disorder can be, but also acknowledges that she has learned a lot through her experiences with her dad.

Have you ever felt scared for someone? Have you been afraid for another's well-being? Do you fear that someone you love is unhappy and may do something unethical and maybe even foolish because they're so depressed they don't know what else to do? Well believe me, I know the feeling!

I'm a seventh-grade, teenage girl who happens to have a dad with bipolar disorder. Trust me, it's not easy! Worrying isn't something I particularly enjoy doing and it can be kind of hard not to worry when your own father is in danger of hurting himself.

Dad Went Away Often

When I was very young, my father, quite a few times, went away for a while. He was actually going to the hospital [rather than] on vacations or business trips, as you may have expected. My daddy often had trouble dealing with the pressures of everyday life. He had to go to the hospital sometimes when his medicine wasn't doing its job, which was to help the chemicals in his mind to even out. People with bipolar disorder have trouble containing their emotions. Sometimes the chemicals in him would make him extremely hyper and excited when just something simple made him happy. Then once the chemicals ran out, his emotions plummeted into a dark and melancholy mood. These mood swings of my dad['s] have even caused him to be suicidal. This makes me extremely worried for him.

Becky Aarons, "Daddy's Disorder," About.com, May 25, 2006. Reproduced by permission.

Yet even with this disorder burdening our family, I have noticed an upside to it all. If my dad didn't have bipolar disorder, I'm not sure he would be the same person he is today. Every little thing that happens or that we do in life adds another building block to the structure of our lives. Even tiny Lego pieces add to our buildings. Without those Lego-sized pieces we would not be exactly the people we are today. The brick-sized pieces of knowledge and experience help a lot, but we all have Legos in our life that we cherish. If my father didn't have bipolar disorder, I wonder if he would still take the time to appreciate the wonders in life.

Dad once explained to me that bipolar disorder is like a train ride. He calls his life "The Bipolar Express," which is sort of a spoof of the movie *The Polar Express*. This silly little spoof actually explains a lot about bipolar disorder. If you've ever seen the movie, you'll notice how the children on the locomotive experience a thrilling and terrifying roller-coaster type trip to the North Pole. My father showed me how similar that crazy train ride and his emotions are. At some point on the ride you are going up and you begin to feel excited and a feeling of pure ecstasy sweeps its warm and happy self into your heart and soul. Then you look over the edge of the summit and time is suspended for a few moments before the coaster releases and is shoved downhill.

A Roller Coaster Ride

To some people that roller coaster drop is worse than others. Some have a 90-degree angle drop like the new Sheikra roller coaster at Busch Gardens in Florida. (I'm a big fan!) Others make the turn around a quick curved slope. Others may have a mild slant while some people have a not-so-mild one. These different slopes . . . and wild trips downhill happen to those with bipolar disorder.

I've personally noticed that dad has had his horrid "Sheikra" [a vertical drop roller coaster] moments, but has also had the not-so-bad mild slants too. Daddy *has* attempted some insane stunts before. My father has tried to hang himself. When he told me this, my heart bled for him. It hurt me terribly to think that this wonderful character with his unique and human foible aspects that I love so much, my own father, even thought about pulling such an idiotic stunt. He told me that what stopped him from going through with it was the sound of my younger brother and me pounding on the garage door and calling for our dad. (We were much younger then. I don't recall it at all.) He said that he had tried a few times to do it, but then realized how stupid he was being when he heard our cries for him.

Dad is an extremely intelligent, kind, caring, loving, hilarious (like Jim Carrey), and just overall awesome person that I love and care deeply for. He may have bipolar disorder and he may have to take medication for it and all, but he is *my* father. He is the one who showed me right from wrong, how to be who I am today and how tough it is to have this disorder. It may be hard to deal with, but we get through it. Whoever said life was easy? Whoever said life was fair? Personally, I prefer it that way!

My Wife Is Bipolar

Kenneth Richard Fox

In this selection, the writer details his wife's descent into bipolar disorder and how she vented her anger by assaulting him. Despite the writer being a doctor, he could not help his wife or their children, and their marriage ended after her final, apparently premeditated attempt on his life. Kenneth Richard Fox, M.D., has more than twenty-five years in private practice, and is chief executive officer of Transglobal Technology, a medical research and development company.

I was driving about 35 miles per hour when, out of the corner of my right eye, I saw a shiny reflection coming directly toward my chest. I grabbed for the forearm and stopped the blade just inches away. My other hand grasped the steering wheel, barely keeping the car from going into a ravine, while my right foot hit the brake.

Wendy and I had met ten years earlier, near the end of my medical residency, and there were times that I thought it had been a match made in heaven. David, our second child, had just arrived when the first signs of Wendy's illness appeared. Our eldest, Kim, was just over three, and the four of us seemed to be the perfect family. Kim was fantastic, and I expected little less from David. I was an eye surgeon and Wendy a speech pathologist. We were, I thought, well established in the community with a nice circle of friends.

Wendy had always been full of energy, positive and forward-looking, highly social, very solid and responsible. People came to know her for these qualities, and I felt very lucky to have her as my wife and best friend.

In the early days after David's birth, Wendy was understandably not quite the same as before; she had two handfuls of responsibility. She began to cancel some professional appointments. Wendy had also been very active in a number of organizations, and, in time, some of that slowed, too.

I was working long hours, so it wasn't until David's first birthday that I realized my wife had developed a habit of sleeping in and leaving his morning care to our live-in nanny. Wendy, who used to insist on doing everything herself, was doing a lot less. She was tired and short-tempered but insisted nothing was wrong. She had a physical examination, and her doctor said she was in good shape.

A couple of years passed. Wendy was still tired and irritable, and she often couldn't sleep through the night. She started seeing psychiatrists. She was diagnosed with severe depression, which may have been triggered by our son's birth. Most of her doctors were reluctant to tell me any more than that because I was the spouse, not the patient, even though I was a professional colleague. Something significant was intruding into our lives, separating us and dividing the family, and her doctors were throwing a cloak of professional silence over it.

The Darkness of Depression

Wendy went through about ten psychiatrists that I knew about. She stopped filing insurance claims, so I had no way to know who she was seeing or any further diagnosis. She was secretive about what her medication was and whether she was taking it. If she was on medication, I couldn't tell the difference. She fluctuated between denying that anything was wrong and being overwhelmed by shame about her problem. When a psychiatrist proposed electroshock therapy or hospitalization, she'd stop seeing him only to find another, searching for one who would tell her that she was okay.

Her father, it turned out, had suffered from major depression, caused by a chemical imbalance in the brain, before he descended into manic depression. This disease, also known as bipolar disorder, tosses the sufferer between extreme highs and lows. Wendy's father died when she was a teenager. She had told me he died of a heart attack, but I later found out he had committed suicide and her family had moved away in part because they felt disgraced.

He used to beat her and perhaps her older sister, Sharon, who also suffered from major depression. Wendy would never admit any of this; from what I was able to understand, she never discussed these issues with her psychiatrists.

Her greatest fear was of becoming "like her father." Her other fear was that she would lose her children. The time came when she sometimes no longer knew what was real. As her depression deepened into manic depression, my wife had become just like her father.

A few of the doctors who didn't mind discussing the problem with me said they had urged Wendy to tell the children, and that she and no one else had to tell them. The point of this had not only to do with her parenting but also her inheritance of this disease. But she never did. She was afraid that if they or anyone else knew, she might lose her family and then even kill herself.

Wendy tried to commit suicide at least once by taking an overdose of pills. I came home from work late one night and found her befuddled and nearly unconscious. I believe if I had not been there, she might not have made it through the night.

Though I was a doctor, there was pitifully little I could do to help my wife, our children, and myself. All of us were suffering.

When she descended into manic depression, Wendy became at times paranoid and delusional and didn't trust anyone. She projected things she thought or did onto other people. As the person closest to her, I became her prime target.

Emotional Seesaw

She was a monolith of anger. In the major depression years, she turned her anger against herself. In the bipolar years, she heaped her anger on others, mostly on those nearest to her.

She accused me and other people of trying to alienate our children from her, steal her money, damage her speech therapy practice, destroy her friendships, drive her crazy, hurt her, and ruin her reputation. Everyone was out to get her.

By the time David was four, Wendy was much less able to work or care for the children. I sold my medical practice shortly thereafter to devote more of my time to this crisis and to taking care of my family. I didn't know what else to do.

I joined a support group for spouses and other family members of manic-depressives and started seeing a therapist, one whom Wendy and I had gone to early on and she had discarded. I wasn't alone anymore; there were others who understood the depth of my despair in this situation. I began to appreciate and understand that others suffer with this same problem all too often.

I began the long, slow process of emerging from "codependence," living the same anguished existence as the partner-patient, like being stuck in the same box with her. The codependent partner needs to break out to stay healthy. I sought to regain my own self-confidence. It was a slow and difficult process. In time, I started to see things more clearly.

After six years of illness, my wife suddenly went into remission. We were able to love again, and life seemed wonderful once more. I began then to think that the manic depression had cured itself.

A year later, the seesaw tipped the other way. The relapse into full-blown bipolar disorder came hard and fast. In the manic phase, Wendy felt better; the black hole of despair went away. There was no stopping her. She was on the move. She got things done. But she was a raving lunatic, which became increasingly apparent to just about everyone she knew. Most of our friends became somewhat more distant. The relatively few friendships that withstood the test of that long period were sweet, indeed, and helped me a lot.

The family therapist we went to at that time threw up his hands, unable to deal with Wendy's anger and abuse. She also had run-ins with authority figures. Wendy crushed anything that got in the way of her systematic denial.

To treat the mania is to risk the return of the depression, a kind of overcorrection. No one in his "wrong mind" would want to do that. Behavior during mania is laced with uncontrollable and dangerous excesses that may include violence, hypersexual activity, insomnia, overworking, overspending, or other extreme behaviors. Manic-depressives often seem normal to people they meet casually. For those who see more of them, the problem is usually unmistakable.

A Prisoner of the Mind

However bad or daunting the major depression had been for me and the children, this mania seemed a hundred times worse. Wendy vented her anger through violence, most often against me but sometimes against our son and other people. In her delusions she believed that almost everyone around her was evil or potentially harmful to her.

After shedding so many psychiatrists along the way, she eventually found a quack psychotherapist who seemed perfectly satisfied to see her for about ten minutes once a month and ask if she was okay. Of course, to herself, she was just fine. This pseudosupport kept her going for a while. He was a far cry from the psychiatrists who wanted to hospitalize her and start major drug or even electroshock therapy. She felt encouraged. The trouble was, this "treatment" was encouraging the monster that was destroying the wife I loved. It is the oddest feeling when this kind of mental illness, this intangible and overpowering force, comes between you and someone you love dearly.

I spent about eleven years in all trying to deal with one phase of her illness or another and seeing our children suffer because of it. When they grew older, she would sometimes tell Kim or even David that she was just "a little down."

Wendy was a prisoner of her brain chemistry. Our kids lived in a house of horrors for much of their formative years and may also have inherited the propensity for the disease from their mother. I was married to the monster that had taken over my wife and my children's mother.

In the last two years of our hellish relationship, my wife physically assaulted me no fewer than twenty-five times. I wound up bruised, scalded, and cut just about every few weeks. These unprovoked attacks even sometimes occurred when I was sleeping. I reported each episode to the police, who wanted to arrest my wife. I refused. I didn't see the criminal justice system as a solution; I didn't see my wife as a criminal but as someone who was very sick. A female police officer who responded to one of my calls told me that her male policeman partner had also been the victim of a petite but physically abusive wife with apparently a very similar illness who wound up in jail.

The twenty-sixth and final violent episode was an apparently premeditated attempt on my life, with a kitchen knife, while I was driving. That was the blow that ultimately ended our marriage. I had to save myself, but I couldn't help her or the children.

No Safety Net

I blame my medical colleagues and those in the other helping professions in part for not being aggressive enough about diagnosing, investigating, and treating this type of mental illness, especially in potentially dangerous cases such as this one was. True, doctors are bound by the patient privilege doctrine, but they are at the same time sometimes the only ones privy to the potential public safety menace that certain of these more violent patients represent. Just as psychiatrists should act to attempt to prevent a suicide, there must be a mechanism for them to suggest to some authority the violent tendencies of certain patients they may see. Only in this manner can these patients be protected from their own destruction or from harming others. In Wendy's case, her extreme denial and the fact that she frequently would change psychiatrists were severe confounding factors in both providing her with more and better treatment and in protecting those around her. However, the level of awareness of psychiatrists in contact professionally with these types of patients must remain very high so that they may see through that cloudy veil worn by patients in denial.

The public "safety net"—police, courts, and social welfare agencies—is also often most unhelpful. Although my own initial reticence to bring my wife into the criminal justice system in the face of her repeated violent episodes was probably not helpful in the long run, once it became quite apparent that there was something drastically wrong, things did not get any better. The U.S. Attorney's office charged with prosecuting Wendy was ultimately cajoled into dismissing the serious assault charge against her because the specter of trying her and in the process interjecting our two children even more into the middle of what was a very ugly situation was highly unappealing.

Taking a singleminded and thoroughly unenlightened view of all of this, the divorce court simply ignored Wendy's significant mental health history, unwilling to require an independent medical evaluation that might have led to an attempt to moderate or modify her violent behavior. That might well have ultimately led to her hospitalization for a trial of medicines or other therapy such as electric shock treatment. That court also was unable to bring itself to separate the potentially dangerous mother from her minor children until sufficient medical remediation of the condition had been accomplished.

By allowing the severe adverse effects of a pathologically angry and violent mother to persist in the home, her two minor children left in contact with her, the children were doomed to suffer long-standing adverse psychological effects. The system makes it virtually impossible to privately bring an action to involuntarily commit these types of individuals. Generally, several psychiatrists have to testify that they have personally seen solid evidence of the worst of the violent behavior; given the denial, the lack of compliance, and proper follow-up in this instance and in others like it this standard is most unlikely to often be met.

I feel strongly that we must do much more for people with severe depression and/or bipolar disorder. When they are thoroughly uncontrolled, we must do something to them to protect both themselves and the rest of us in their midst. Year by year we learn more about this common but sometimes violent disorder and the havoc that it visits upon individuals, families, and society. Doctors involved in treating these patients need to be as proactive as possible. Judges ought to be further educated about the horrible potential consequences of this condition; the law must ... require them to act in the best interests of minor children but also protect those patients and loved ones around them from the ravages of this disease. The police need to understand more about bipolar disorder and its many faces; social service networks that interface with these people also should act in a more inspired and proactive fashion in their dealings with them.

Raising a Child with Bipolar Disorder

Debbie Orkin

In this selection, the author talks about raising her oldest son, who, at a very young age, displayed bipolar symptoms and even tried to kill himself. She recounts the daily frustrations and moments of hope and acknowledges that the battle with her son's illness has made her family and faith stronger. Debbie Orkin is a mother of five and the founder of a support group for families of children with mental illness.

When I was a child, there were three things that made me feel frightened: photographs and film footage from the early 1970's (a whole story in itself), severe weather, and being around people that suffered from a mental illness. As I grew older, the first two "fears" dissipated, but the third one stuck with me, although with less severity than it had in my youth.

Afraid of Mental Illness

The first encounter I remember having with someone who had a mental illness was when I was in elementary school. I was in second grade and the school had a program for kids/ young adults with different types of mental and physical disabilities. My first real memory was of a young man who was probably about fifteen or sixteen at the time. He had a severe mental disability. For whatever reason, he was always roaming the hallways by himself, and if another child was there without a teacher (going to restroom, office, etc.), he would chase them down the hall, screaming whatever it was he was trying to say. Inevitably, this led to many tears and fears on my part, to the point that I didn't want to leave the classroom alone. As the years went by, I overcame the fear, but still felt uncomfortable around people with mental illness.

When my oldest son was born, we were so excited. It was pure bliss ... until we brought him home. I nursed because I thought that it would be the healthiest for him, but he had a voracious appetite and I couldn't keep up. I had to quit nursing when he was three months old. During his first six months, he had a terrible time settling down after a feeding. My husband would have to walk around with him for what seemed like hours. As a baby, he had problems entertaining himself, was very cranky, and just all-around difficult. But we didn't realize it until our second son was born and caring for him was a piece of cake. Now you may be thinking our first son had a developmental disability, but that was not the case. He reached all his milestones, some one month early, and he could speak a little on a telephone at about fifteen months. So we thought that we had been blessed with a very bright child. Healthy and bright—what more could a mom want?

Strange Behavior Patterns

As he got older though, we started noticing behavior patterns. At first we thought he was just spoiled. Whenever he didn't get his way, he would have a complete fit. I remember when he was two and a half, he threw a dining room chair at me because we didn't have any Raisin Bran. Our pediatrician sent us to a child psychologist so we could try to learn how to deal with his behaviors, but it is extremely hard to diagnose a two-year-old.

The major problems started when he was four. Our son was enrolled in a boys school that has about 800 students K-12. His teachers kept calling, telling us about all of the issues they were having with him in school. He was constantly hurting other kids, not listening, making inappropriate comments, etc., so we went to see another child psychologist. The doctor felt that it was a behavioral issue, and by being strict with our son and challenging him intellectually, he would straighten out. So for the next two years, we tried to go on with our daily lives. It wasn't easy but we somehow managed, and during that time he became the older brother to another two brothers, making him the oldest of four. And then, in March of three years ago, our whole world was turned around.

A Turn for the Worse

It started on [the Jewish holiday] Purim. He was aggressive, running away, and very explosive. My neighbor found him one day after school in the school parking lot down the street in the middle of carpool time. We just didn't know what to do anymore. We saw that these were not normal behaviors. We spoke to a relative of mine who works for a pediatric "health system" in our city. He referred us to a psychiatrist and we had an appointment the next day. We met with her and we talked about our son and his issues, and at first she thought it was ADHD [attention-deficit hyperactivity disorder]. I was so happy. Finally, we knew, or at least we thought that we knew, what was wrong with our son. She prescribed the usual Ritalin, and for the first day, it was great. I felt like I had my son back. He told me he never felt that relaxed in his whole life. Well, that changed quickly over the next few days when he threatened to jump out of my bedroom window, then climbed out the living room window and tried to run away. We went back to the psychiatrist and she saw right away what it really was. My beautiful, brilliant, funny, compassionate son was literally climbing her bookcases, screaming like a wild animal. That was the day we got the diagnosis of Bipolar Disorder.

A chemical imbalance in the brain that causes severe mood swings, combinations of mania with depression, thoughts of grandiosity, bipolar disorder is different in children than adults. When an adult with bipolar becomes manic, they will generally do things like go on shopping sprees and get themselves into loads of debt, or write hundreds of pages of manuscript that make no sense whatsoever. But in pediatric bipolar, the mania is different. The child tends to become extremely aggressive, violent, have feelings of being the king of the world.

Spinning out of Control

For the next week or so, I was walking around like a zombie. I couldn't eat, sleep, or get through much of the day without crying. We were completely overrun. The whole family felt very guilty. We thought that our son could control his rages. He looked like he was turning them on and off. In reality, he couldn't. When I was pregnant with him, I would pray that he should be healthy. When we do that, we usually mean physical health, not mental. I became very angry and frustrated and didn't know how to deal with my feelings. As time went on, I realized that there were better ways to deal with my frustration. I joined an online support group and got a counselor to help me sort out all of my feelings.

During the first months after his diagnosis, our son went through a myriad of medications. Some worked and some didn't. Many had some pretty bad side effects. It wasn't until the summer that we found something that worked, or at least we thought it did. During the first week of July, our son spiraled very quickly. We made the decision to hospitalize him. It was a complete nightmare and it took an entire day of phone calls to two different hospitals and our insurance company before we were able to admit him.

My husband saw that I was falling apart over this, and forbade me to go with him to admit our son. I was completely racked with guilt, although the decision to admit him was for the best. Watching my son that day was like watching a wild animal. It was also very difficult because as much as we tried to explain it, he didn't understand what to expect when he finally got to the unit. My son was convinced he would be lying around all day watching television, like he has seen from visiting others in the hospital or a nursing home. When we first got to the unit, which is locked because it is a psych unit, we had our bags checked to make sure that we weren't bringing in any "contraband." He was not allowed to bring any glass with him, such as picture frames, and no sharp objects or belts.

When we went to visit him the next day, he seemed to have figured it out. I remember sitting in the hallway crying and watching two staff members carry him into a "timeout room." It was just too much for any one person to handle. I just kept thinking, G-d, please get us through this. Please help our son get healthy again. It took a lot of praying, and faith that everything would turn out okay (whatever that meant). He stayed inpatient for a week, but had to be readmitted four days later due to extremely violent behavior. This included trying to swing on the blade of a running ceiling fan, choking me and beating me. All this, seemingly, because I said "no" to his request.

We got through the rest of the summer as best we could. It was very stressful on our other sons, especially our second son who was five years old at the time. He had unfortunately become a human punching bag to his big brother. When we discussed with them what was going on with our oldest, our five-year-old was jumping for joy. That is how unsafe he felt in our home. It's a terrible feeling to know that you just can't keep your children safe, especially from a sibling. When school started that fall, our son went back to school. We explained to the rabbi and his teacher what was going on with him. Things seemed to be going well considering he spent two weeks in a psych unit, didn't go to any summer camp, and had to adjust to going back to school (which can be a trauma in itself).

An Incident at School

But then we found out that there was an incident during the second or third week of school. Pretty serious in their minds, overreaction in ours. We had a meeting, which included the psychiatrist. The bottom line was that the school didn't want to deal with our son. The principal decided our son should be home for two days, and they wanted a dose of meds to be added and given during the school day. The school wanted guarantees we couldn't give. In the end, we didn't add any meds because we knew that wasn't the answer. We just shifted the doses to appease the school. All it did was make our son fall asleep in class. I was very angry. We pay a lot of tuition money for my children to learn, not to take naps.

It was actually a very nerve-racking time. My husband and I were afraid that the school was setting the stage for kicking our son out. We even went so far as to look at a Jewish special needs school in our community. The problem was that it didn't sound like they would want to accept him. Our son is very bright, and most of the kids in their school are not able to learn on their grade level. The school was afraid that our son would get bored and act out, which would not be a good situation. But after much discussion and prayer, especially prayer, things in school calmed down.

Unfortunately, his behaviors at home did not. When our son first went into the hospital last summer, my husband asked me what my biggest fear was. I told him it was that our son would try to kill himself. Maybe not today, tomorrow, or next month, but maybe five or ten years down the road. I really didn't think that it would happen when he was seven years old.

The Threat of Suicide

It was [the Jewish Day of Atonement] Yom Kippur night. Of course, it was about five minutes after everybody left for services. I wasn't really paying attention to what my sons were doing. I mean, how much trouble could these boys make? They were all in the living room with me, getting into their pajamas, goofing around. I was feeding the baby, reading a book, ignoring my children. For whatever reason, I decided to look up. I saw my eldest son trying to strangle himself with his belt. At first it seemed like an impulse, but once I got it off him and we talked, I realized that this was something he really wanted to do. He told me that he was killing himself because he didn't want to live anymore. My heart almost stopped beating. How would a seven-year-old know about these things? He told me he always felt stupid (this is a child who taught himself to play chess when he was four), that nobody loved him (we tell him that we love him everyday), that he has no friends (even after his incident in school someone invited him to sleep over for [the Jewish Day of Rest] Shabbat). I saw from this conversation, through many tears of his and mine, that he really has a low self-esteem and is slightly delusional. We didn't put him into the hospital that night, although we should have. We knew that if we did, he would end up being there for all of [the Jewish Holiday] Sukkot, and none of us wanted that.

For the next couple of weeks, we were walking on eggshells, trying to keep him somewhat sedated, until after Sukkot when he tried to strangle himself again. Then we put him back in the hospital. Sometimes I wonder if G-d is playing a cruel trick on us. How could He do this? But, I realized, whether I like it or not, it is making us stronger. I have a friend whose daughter is autistic. She told me the worst thing people could say to you is the oft common saying, "G-d only gives you what you can handle." It's not true. There are plenty of times we can't handle it. Times when we want to just walk away. But perhaps the reason G-d gives us challenges like this is to make our belief and trust in Him that much stronger.

Finding Strength

When we felt that we had hit rock bottom, when we couldn't possibly handle any more, we decided to finally be proactive with what we were dealing with, rather than solely reactive. It [was] at that point that we really started the process of getting help for ourselves. Through advocating for our son, and meeting other families, we saw that we weren't the only ones in our community dealing with these struggles. We decided to start our own support group. Our group really just started during the summer and we have a core group of about six or seven families. There are three main goals of the group: 1) providing basic support for the families, 2) educating the community about mental illness to help take away some of the stigma, and 3) providing a social outlet for families. We meet about once a month, and hope to eventually open ourselves up to include any family in our community who has a child with a serious mental illness.

For many years, we hoped that this problem would be solved. That it would just somehow go away. We have now accepted that taking care of our son is a daily struggle that could continue for the rest of his life. Our son's days, and our lives in general, are very unpredictable due to this horrific disease, but for now, this is what we have. We, including our other sons, have somewhat figured out what sets him off. Okay, we are generally walking on eggshells around him, but until he stabilizes, we see that this is our life. He is doing well in his school, which is a special school for emotionally disturbed children. His school is a level five school, meaning it is the most restrictive environment within the public school system. They work on a point system as a positive reinforcement. The school is a real ego stroker, if you know what I mean, and it has been really good for my son's self esteem. But it is also strict in what it does or does not allow. If you mess up, you are in the resource room, and if you get violent, you go to the isolation room. Most importantly, the school accepts him for who he is. And he attends a learning program once a week for special needs boys at one of our local [rabbinical school] yeshivot.

Connecting to others in similar situations also reinforced something we always knew in our minds but had to really feel in our hearts and souls. This challenge has shown us the importance and need for true faith and belief in our Creator. He is the one who is truly guiding us through our lives. There is no question that if He gave us our situation, He can also give us the means and strength to deal with it. And every day, we see more and more that there can be light at the end of what has been a very dark tunnel.

And with time, I can see the progress that we have all made. A few years back I would not have envisioned that I could be a source of strength and optimism to others. But I have been, and that has inspired me to believe that we will make it through this. And as hard as it can be to see at times, underneath the anger and illness is a beautiful child, a precious soul that we have been blessed to have as our son. There is no question that we have faced many challenges and, unfortunately, may have more to come. But we also believe that we will somehow have the strength to face them, and one day, overcome them as well.

Our Marriage Became Constant Chaos

Y. Euny Hong

The writer, diagnosed with bipolar disorder, recounts her whirlwind courtship with her husband. She describes how she came to realize that her new husband was also suffering from bipolar disorder, and his erratic and destructive behavior that eventually destroyed their marriage. Y. Euny Hong has written for many magazines and newspapers and is the author of the novel Kept.

Between January and May of 2006, my husband, Leopold, attempted suicide four times, at nearly regular intervals of five weeks. In June, he disappeared for a month. When he re-emerged, he announced he was quitting me, his job, and the city in which we lived. He was going to teach at a high school in Appalachia.

Just two years prior, we'd met at a mutual friend's birthday party and secluded ourselves on the fire escape, smoking. I lived in New York; he was in D.C. The following Saturday, we talked on the phone for six hours. I visited him two weeks later. Over the weekend, he asked me to move in with him; by Sunday night, we'd picked out the names of our unborn children. Like Tristan and Isolde, we were bewitched by each other. Leopold proposed to me four weeks after that.

A Stormy Courtship

My friends thought it was empetuous of me to go along with this breakneck courtship—especially since the ink was barely dry on my divorce from my first husband—but I could not be dissuaded. This was my lifelong image of what love should be like, and I was eager to start afresh.

Y. Euny Hong, "Living with a Crazy Husband," *Marie Claire*, December 1, 2008. Reproduced by permission.

Only later, after meeting with Leopold's shrinks, did I understand that this wasn't romance—it was a disease. Specifically, it was a symptom of the manic side of "manic-depressive illness," also known as bipolar disorder.

Like many bipolar sufferers, Leopold had gone his whole life without being diagnosed. The mania was seen as part of his personality. He was a consummate romantic, showering me with flowers and surprises. We loved each other to excess. He would say he missed me if we were in two separate rooms of the apartment.

Where I should have seen signs of a problem, I saw lovable quirks. Leopold was able to envision the distant future (like knowing what those unborn children would major in at college). But the short-term future—anything more than a few months in advance—eluded him. He had written the first 50 pages of a novel seven years earlier—but he'd bristle if I pressed him about finishing it.

I attributed tendencies like these to a combination of Gen-X apathy and traditional male immaturity. He once told me, "I'm the best damn writer in the world." But he was unable to take concrete steps to test his abilities. (I later learned that hyperconfidence is also a sign of mania.)

Irrational Behavior

What he couldn't plan for tomorrow, Leopold had no trouble determining for today: Shortly after our wedding, he decided to buy a car. His parents offered him advice on finding the best deal, negotiating the financing rate, shopping around. Leopold left for the dealership at 2 P.M. At 5 P.M. he drove home with a new car. His parents gave him a tongue-lashing for his impulsiveness. He flopped on the bed and told me, "I want to hurt myself."

All honeymoons end; in our case, it ended almost before it began. We often fought about his job, which required him to spend half his time in a Middle Eastern country that was on the State Department's unsafe list. He said, "Everything in my life has been leading up to this job. If you deny me this, you deny me everything." I didn't know how to respond to that kind of extreme, unchecked zeal.

The funny thing is, for most of the time we were together, it was my mental health with which we were preoccupied, not his. Full disclosure: I am bipolar, too. I was diagnosed with bipolar type II years ago. In type II, the manic and depressive episodes are distinct from each other and relatively easy to recognize. It was strangely fortunate that my depression was so pronounced—I cried constantly, had an irrational social phobia, and didn't brush my hair for months at a time—because it allowed me to seek help at an early stage.

Leopold, meanwhile, was bipolar type I. His manic episodes were much more pronounced than the depressive ones. Many bipolar sufferers don't seek treatment because the manic side, which in mild stages resembles euphoria, is actually enjoyable. But euphoria can be terribly dangerous. Bipolar people are two to three times more likely to attempt suicide than those suffering from regular depression. They are also, say studies, more likely to complete their attempts.

A Suicide Attempt

The real signs of trouble occurred about a month before our first wedding anniversary. Leopold had been passed over for a promotion in favor of someone less qualified. He was overseas at the time, so I didn't directly witness the effect the news had on him.

But in January, two weeks after he returned, he made his first suicide attempt. I found him sitting in front of the computer with a plastic bag over his head. Thirty days after that, he reached for my bag of medications, looking for something to OD on. These attempts were precipitated by our fights, which allowed the blame to fall on my shoulders.

Thirty-six days later, he opened my bottle of Ambien, the prescription sleep aid, and put half the pills in his mouth. I tried to dial 911; he ripped the phone out of my hands. I went to the neighbors' place, hoping they would let me use their phone. No one answered. Leopold finally allowed me to call the police, who showed up a few minutes later at our apartment. They told me not to say anything; they wanted to hear what had happened from Leopold. Suddenly, Leopold became serene and stoic. "I'm sorry she made you come out here," he said to the policemen. "She really overreacted."

The police asked how many pills he had taken. I spilled the remaining pills and estimated that he had taken about half. "I spit them out," said Leopold, pointing to a plastic cup, which contained a largely indistinct chalky sludge mixed with blood.

The cops drove us to the hospital in separate cars. At the hospital waiting room, I stepped out to call a doctor friend of mine. She was alarmed but assured me that Ambien was among the safer sleep medications and that it was fast-acting, so if Leopold wasn't asleep already, he probably hadn't consumed that many. Relieved, I reported this to Leopold, who said, "Now I feel really stupid. I should have tried to take something else."

I asked him to write down the reasons he felt it was necessary to do this. He returned the paper to me, and it read, "It was the only recourse I had to stave off your attacks." A few minutes later, he passed me a piece of paper on which he'd drawn a tic-tac-toe grid and wanted me to play. I refused. "OK, we'll play hangman," he said.

The attending physician thought the suicide attempt was a prank and let Leopold go with a stern warning.

My Husband in a Mental Hospital

Several days later, Leopold went to see his shrink. He called to tell me that his doctor was alarmed and was driving him to a mental hospital.

For the next week, I visited the hospital every day. Visiting hours were hellish. The hospital staff checked my bag for caffeinated beverages, sweets, plastic bags. In this environment, it was assumed that all substances could be used for self-harm. The cutlery was plastic and was counted carefully; shaving was permitted only in the presence of an orderly. Leopold was there for just under a week. He was always heavily sedated; I never knew calmness could look so creepy. But I couldn't deny that he seemed more at peace.

I was disturbed by how at home he was. He told me how the art-therapy teacher was impressed with his work, and showed me one of the drawings—a sketch of me with devil's horns. I cried and asked why he showed me that. He seemed genuinely surprised by my reaction, saying he just wanted to show me his art. He spoke with a distant contentedness about how he hoped to stay friends with the other patients, how well-liked he was by the staff, and how he was afraid to re-enter the real world.

His family was in disbelief. "Leopold was always such a happy boy," his mother said on the phone. "I don't understand what could have happened to him in the last year." How could the class clown be suicidal? What kind of woman ruins two marriages before age 33? All fingers pointed to me.

Getting Out

I never considered ending the marriage. I knew that we'd have to take turns caring for each other during our respective rough patches. If anything, doomed love was romantic.

Two days after Leopold was released from the hospital, I met up with my friend Gerald. When Gerald asked where Leopold was, I said he was at his stand-up-comedy class, which was true. Then I broke down and told him about Leopold's hospital stay.

"So he's not really at a stand-up-comedy class," said Gerald.

"Oh, he is. That part wasn't a lie."

Gerald furrowed his eyebrows. "You don't think it's weird that he wants to go to a comedy class two days after leaving a mental hospital?"

No. I didn't. It was the manic pattern I'd come to recognize.

For a few weeks after his release from the hospital, things were returning to calm. I became involved in Leopold's recovery, enforcing early bedtimes and other regular habits, as routines are important for bipolar sufferers. He even made progress on his novel; what he wrote during that period was exquisite.

But it didn't last. Forty-one days after Leopold's third suicide attempt, he contacted an ex-girlfriend behind my back. I found his timing callous. Saying, "I'm the one who takes care of you," I threw my wedding ring down the sewer (remember, I have manic episodes, too). Leopold disappeared.

Worried about his mental stability, I called his friends to ask if they'd heard from him. They made it very clear that they thought I had forfeited my right to know anything about him.

I found out later that Leopold had made another suicide attempt. A week after that, he'd gone onstage for an open-mike night at a comedy club.

A month later, after the barest of contact about purely practical matters, Leopold returned home to announce that he was abandoning his "previous" life to teach school in rural Appalachia. Repeating one of his favorite statements, he looked at me resolutely and said, "Everything in my life has been leading to this path."

It's been two years since we parted ways, and we've had limited contact. I still wonder what role I may have played in unleashing the most extreme form of his disease. I hate to say it, but it was one of the cleanest breakups I've ever had—it was simply too shocking to hold on to sentiment. Now, I am wary of overly romantic gestures, which is sad. But prudent.

Dating a Bipolar Woman

Justin Clark

The writer of this article finds himself attracted to a bipolar woman because of her illness, and not despite it. Enthralled by her exuberance and directness, he soon finds out that his life is governed by her obsessive needs, and that her disorder won't leave any space for normalcy. Justin Clark has written for L.A. Weekly, Psychology Today, *and* Black Book.

At the end of my first date with Sara, she moved in with me.

You might think the date was extraordinary. It wasn't. We'd gone to a Hollywood hamburger stand and gabbed about bands and writers for four hours. Until that night, we'd only spoken on the phone a few times. It didn't matter. By the time the ice in my soda had melted, I'd fallen in love.

Sara was twenty-seven, and what people used to call a wag: smart, quick-witted, encyclopedic. She could recount every failed Everest expedition in mesmerizing detail—the sort of a talent I would expect of a rock climber, not someone who'd never gone camping. I kept wondering why no one had snapped her up. Then I found out.

"There's something you should know about me," she said, a couple of hours into the date. "I hope it doesn't scare you off."

Panicked thoughts raced through my mind. A jealous ex? An STD? I tried to remember if I'd sipped from her drink.

"I'm bipolar," she said.

"Good," I replied.

Bipolar People Were Interesting

This was the odd humor Sara and I had already established, but I wasn't entirely joking. I'd had several close bipolar

Justin Clark, "Love Rollercoaster," Nerve.com, January 28, 2008. Reproduced by permission.

friends, and had once been in a long-term relationship with a bipolar woman, Nyla, whom I still consider the smartest person I'd ever met. From a distance, I'd seen how much energy it took Nyla to keep her episodes under control: weekly doctor's visits, blood tests, complicated regimens of medications.

And yet for all their problems, my bipolar buddies had always kept things interesting. My friend Jerome was hired one summer to drive a van full of rich and annoying European teenagers across the country. Somewhere in the Midwest, without telling the kids or his employer or anyone else where he was going, he simply got out at a gas station and walked away. "I was bored," he told me. Irresponsible, yes, but hilarious.

I didn't hear Sara's story until later, but it didn't have many funny parts. Her condition was rooted in a childhood depression that began when her father died suddenly of stomach cancer. At eighteen, she enrolled in the Ivy League university she'd dreamt of attending since childhood, and within a semester, was incapacitated by depression; she dropped out and returned to L.A. Suicide attempts followed. Then came her diagnosis, and years of experimenting with different psychiatric drugs until her doctors found the magic combination. Sidelined for years, she was finally looking forward again: doing PR for a record label and working part-time toward her bachelor's degree.

Moving In Together

How could you not admire such a person? When I looked at Sara, I felt inspiration, not pity. And even though I'm not the type to plunge quickly into relationships, I was convinced I was in love. I invited her back to my place. Aside from a quick trip to clean out her studio apartment a few weeks later, she never went home.

"Of the two of us," I told her as we lay happily in bed, "I must be the crazier one."

Nine months later I stood over her pale, unconscious body, frantically dialing 911 for the first time in my life.

You could compile an entire book of quotes comparing love to madness. But of all the psychological issues in the *DSM-IV* [*Diagnostic and Statistical Manual of Mental Disorders*], only one really resembles the experience of love. "An illness that is unique in conferring advantage and pleasure," writes Dr. Kay Jamison in one of the most famous memoirs of bipolar illness, *An Unquiet Mind*. It's easy to confuse love with mania, Jamison says. The trouble is that love is fleeting. There's no cure for bipolar.

The popular caricature of the disease—people swinging rapidly between happiness and sadness—isn't the whole story. Most of us may have been unhappy enough at one time or another to recognize a fit of depression, but the other half of the disease (the mania that leads to everything from religious fervor to shopaholism to insatiable libido) is much harder to fathom. For instance, hypomania, which is a mild form of mania characterized by enviable productivity, can lead to what is called a "mixed state," in which the bipolar individual is both miserable and energetic enough to do something about it. Before [Sara] had found an effective combination of meds, she drove halfway across the country in a mixed state, buying expensive clothes and jewelry for herself, with the goal of committing suicide when she reached California. Fortunately, her mania dissipated before she made it there.

Like such behavior, love is nonsensical. All relationships suffer from irrationality, which is why they can be particularly susceptible to the ups and downs of bipolar. The most obvious problem is the wild swings in libido: one week your partner wants sex all the time—maybe too often—and the next they've got the sexual impulses of a Buddhist monk. With both Nyla and Sara, I never knew what sort of response my advances would receive. And after sex, when I thought we'd both enjoyed ourselves, sometimes [Sara] would burst into tears. "What's wrong?" I'd whisper, to which she'd cryptically reply, "I feel overwhelmed."

Sara's life was a constant battle against entropy [disorganization]. While most of us are bored by too much routine, Sara was obsessive about hers, and as her boyfriend, I found myself joining her in it. I, who have never liked TV, started watching hours of it with her every night. Infatuated with cleaning products, Sara taught me the joys of repetitive household maintenance. It took her all day to clean the bathroom, and when she was done, she would begin all over again. "It's better than watching TV, isn't it?" she'd say, as if these predictable tasks were the only options.

Our relationship became defined by obsessive routine, something that might normally have made me feel antsy and restless. But because Sara clung to the structure so fervently, I followed her lead. I began to drop off the social map. The parameters of our life together drew further and further inward, until we were living in a tiny, airtight box created by the quirks of her disorder. I became not only her enabler, but her progeny as well.

A Misunderstood Disorder

This probably isn't how most people picture bipolar disorder. Yet despite this, more people than ever think they know what bipolar is—a mixed blessing for those who suffer from it. This is partially thanks to the ubiquity of advertisements for medications like Abilify and Zyprexa, and partially due to diagnoses, which have doubled over the last decade. A 1997 National Mental Health Association survey found that more than two-thirds of Americans had limited or no knowledge of the disease; almost a decade later, eight out of ten Americans think they know what bipolar disorder is. Everyone from disgraced *New York Times* reporter Jayson Blair to Debra LaFave, the high-school teacher convicted of seducing her fourteen-year-old student, has employed the bipolar defense. And if they don't trumpet it as the explanation for their misdeeds, media experts are happy to do so on their behalf. Without ever having met her, Fox News contributor Dr. Keith Ablow all but diagnosed Britney Spears on air this month [March 2008]. "I would put on the list of possibilities a mood disorder like bipolar," he said, further cementing it as the official catch-all for crazy people.

"There is never a story or scene with healthy, happy bipolars because even though that type comprises the bulk of the population, it doesn't sell and isn't exciting," says a bipolar woman who maintains a blog about bipolar disorder called Weird Cake. "Top this off with sensational misinformation from people like Oprah, and you build a population that fears us and looks for us in dark corners."

As a result, half of all American adults say they wouldn't date a bipolar person. Back when I dated Sara, I wasn't one of them. I'd read in Psychology Today that ninety percent of marriages involving a bipolar person end in divorce, but I figured that statistic applied to couples who were ill-informed about the illness, people who weren't prepared to meet it head-on. I also ascribed the figure to reporting bias: there were plenty of people out there who were bipolar and lived drama-free lives, and thus never made it into the statistics. Yet even with everything I knew about the disorder, I still constantly discovered new challenges, as basic as figuring out who my partner really was, as mundane as whether I should say something when she started cleaning the toilet bowl for the third time in a row.

The Line Between Personality and Illness

Even in the most even-keeled people, dating can be a crisis between ideality and reality. We're constantly told that the key to successful dating is to be yourself. However, "when you have a psychiatric illness, it's a part of you," says a bipolar Brit[on] who keeps a pseudonymous blog: Social Anxiety and

Bipolar Diary of Annie. "You cannot tell where your personality ends and the illness begins."

Locating this gulf between personality and illness often falls to the significant other. "I find it difficult to realize when my daydreams cross a line into unhealthy hypomania," says Annie. "This is where I rely on my friends to put me right and stop me from getting carried away." The role of caregiver can strain any relationship. While Sara took her meds and saw her psychiatrist faithfully, she also neglected her physical health, leaving me with the choice between watching her eat nothing but popsicles all day long, or nagging her about it.

And as anyone would, she resented it when I played nutritionist. I eventually decided the only way to preserve the relationship was to let her do what she wanted. As her physical health seemed to deteriorate, I resisted temptations to call her doctor. But according to David Oliver, I should have. Oliver, who is not a psychiatrist, runs one of the Internet's most popular sites on bipolar disorder. Bipolar Central. He launched his bipolar consulting business because he was dissatisfied with the professional care his bipolar mother received.

"There's a huge flaw in the system," says Oliver. "They give you fifteen minutes at the doctor, they forget to tell you there are ten to twelve different meds, or to warn you about the side effects you're experiencing."

Trying to Do the Right Thing

That lack of professional supervision means people in relationships with bipolar individuals must step outside the normal boundaries, according to Oliver—communicating with your boyfriend's doctor behind his back, for instance. Such actions have saved lives; they've also violated trust, and in the end, I found myself unable to tell where the line separating those two requirements was. "It has been my experience that some people [with a bipolar partner] use the disorder as their immunity card," says Danielle. "Nothing in the relationship is their fault because they're dating or married to a bipolar person." My relationship with Sara was filled with gray areas—the popsicle issue, for instance—in which I could never figure out the right thing to do.

Which is why some bipolar people prefer to date others with the same disorder. Thirty-seven-year-old librarian James Leftwich struggled for years with relationships because of his schizoaffective disorder—essentially bipolar coupled with schizophrenia's delusions or hallucinations. Tired of being misunderstood by a population generally unfamiliar with his condition, he created . . . one of the few dating websites for the mentally ill. In four years, he says, the site has helped produce countless relationships and at least six marriages. But even for someone with a similar illness, another person's mental health is not an easy thing to be responsible for, and Leftwich says even he isn't sure he would use his own website right now. "Personally, I'm in a frame of mind where I'm not sure I want someone with a mental illness," he says.

On the other hand, an issue like bipolar disorder may encourage a healthy sense of compassion. When twenty-eight-year-old software engineer Jil told her husband about her illness on their very first date, she was happy that he seemed a little bewildered and had lots of questions—it meant he cared. "I also wanted to be a better person because of him, and when I feel no other reason to swallow those pills that stabilize my mood, I do it for his sake, not just my own," says Jil.

Taken Away

It was a sunny Saturday morning. Just a few minutes earlier I'd been lying on the couch, reading one of the self-help books Sara had given me to help ease us through our crumbling relationship. Then, without warning, she stumbled out of the bathroom and collapsed on the floor. I think I would have lost it had she not regained consciousness a minute or so later, or if the paramedics had not arrived as quickly as they did. After

I gave them the names of Sara's medications and watched them load her into the ambulance, I called her mother, a woman I'd only spoken to a few times. She received the news almost serenely. It wasn't the first time her daughter had been whisked off to the hospital.

Sara's wasn't an overdose, or a suicide attempt—at least, not an overt one. I'd known Sara was severely anemic, that her pills had made her stomach bleed. For months I'd asked her what her doctors were doing about it, and she'd given me cheerful answers about iron infusions and blood transplants. I no longer believed her, but I wasn't sure what I was supposed to do. I researched her medications and learned all sorts of frightening things. One of them wasn't even indicated for her disorder; it was an epilepsy medication that the drug companies encouraged psychiatrists to use off-label.

But it was difficult for me to voice my reservations about her care. Sara liked hospitals. She loved [the television sitcom] *Scrubs*. She admired doctors, detested any criticism of the medical system, and talked about her psychiatrist as if he were a best friend. When she spent a night at a sleep-study clinic (she thought she was narcoleptic), she talked about it as if it were a slumber party. She kept getting into fender benders from falling asleep on the freeway, yet still insisted on driving to volunteer at the hospital that had saved her after her suicide attempt. It was more than simple gratitude, she admitted; the hospital's rituals made her feel safe and comfortable. She talked about it the way other people talk about visiting their grandparents.

Losing Trust

When I told Sara what I'd learned about her medications, she told me she would rather die than get off of them, and pointed out that she knew the cost of them better than I did. She couldn't remember words, for instance—she who had wanted to be a writer. But those pills had given her a reason to live.

Did I know better than her doctors did? No, I supposed I didn't. I knew that for us to have a healthy relationship, though, I needed to trust her. The trouble was, I no longer did. At that moment, I decided I couldn't stay with Sara any longer.

That day, when I got to the hospital, I found her looking happier than I'd ever seen her. I was baffled. Five minutes earlier the doctor had informed us that her life was in danger if she didn't find some way to fix her anemia. But she seemed at peace now. That was the worst part about it—in her hospital gown, sitting up on her austere gurney bed, she looked as if she were finally at home.

I have my own theory about relationships with the bipolar: the successful ones are those in which the relationship simply isn't in competition with the disease. Sara seemed to regard the illness as a more intimate part of her than I could ever understand—not just a profoundly affecting experience, the way other serious diseases are, but almost the entire essence of her existence. In the end, I simply wanted there to be more.

Medications Can Wreak Havoc on Your Mind and Body

Pole to Polar

Despite taking several medications over the years, the author describes that it has been impossible to get relief from her disorder's symptoms, and details the side effects from the medication she has tried. She notes with frustration that even though medication stabilizes her, it makes her feel worn out and apathetic.

I think I expected too much from medication.

I didn't want to rely on drugs to fix me, being that I believed (and still do, especially in the case of antidepressants and childhood behavioural problems that are too easily diagnosed as "mental illness") that medication was overprescribed and nothing but a crutch for a weary mind to rest upon. But I figured, if I'm not that ill, medication won't hurt me. It'll only be for a month or two.

I was prescribed Lithium and had read a lot about people who took it and just snapped back into life. That will be me, I thought greedily. So I took the pills. Lithium was a disaster.

Well, disaster is putting it strongly. Putting it mildly, Lithium was not my drug. I felt like I was being punished for something. First of all, I wasn't allowed my own stash for about six weeks. The Crisis Team administered the doses and, I was reassured, this awful sickness would pass. I took Zopiclone too but would still wake up in the night shaking and sick. I could tell you every detail of the carpet in the bedroom because I had spent so much time with my head over the edge retching. And the toilet bowl and I became acquainted. I was sick, all the time, dazed, dandering through smoke and sepia and shaking constantly. I slurred my words, I often couldn't remember my name. It wrecked my sex drive. . . .

Losing a Job

To top it off, it didn't help me. Even with Lithium and copious amounts of zonked out Zopiclone sleep, I lapsed into a manic episode and found myself unemployed.

I'm beginning to think that I have given up on medications too soon because of how terrible I found Lithium. . . . I'm not crawling into pits or spinning from heights but my moods are flip-flopping all over the place, taking my motivation, my emotions, my mind with them. Huge mood swings are awful, but the constant cycling is also taking its toll on me.

It's been over two years, a lot of drugs and a lot of not being well.

Before I was formally diagnosed I was given Carbamazepine and Olanzapine to "calm me down". Shorthand for, "manic" but we're not telling her. I took Carbamazepine during one of the most sustained manic and psychotic episodes of my life. I felt totally pissed. I gained a shitload of weight on Olanzapine and couldn't function.

I gave up on Depakote because my hair was falling out, I was constantly knackered [tired], I gained a lot of weight and it really wasn't helping me. I also felt nauseous on that too. It doesn't help that the dose I was on (1,000 mg [milligrams]) was like swallowing two large lilos [air mattresses] a day. Those pills are huge.

I took Lamictal. On one dose, 150 mg, I was a zombie, absolutely dead. On another, 100 mg, nothing worked. I stayed on Lamictal for ages, but then took my overdose and now get Vietnam flashbacks when I even think of Lamictal. I also kept getting rashes (I'm not sure they were related, [as] when I become stressed, I get rashes) and withdrawing from it was hellish.

Medications Had Severe Side Effects

Then there were the antidepressants, each one a complete failure, if you define failure as kicking me into the most raging of dysphorias. They are, in general, now off the menu for me.

I continued to take Seroquel, [and] I still do. That should have been the first medication I chucked into the Thames as it was largely the main culprit in my ballooning bottom, bosom and belly. But it was the sleep. Oh god the sleep. I slept like the dead. Sixteen hours a day at least. After ten years of never sleeping, this was so enticing. Now I hate that. I hate how much I sleep. I hate that if I don't go to bed immediately after taking my Seroquel, paralysis kicks in and I start to feel paranoid and unsafe. It does help mania and anxiety but mostly because I sleep so much that it's nigh on impossible for me to be seriously manic unless I stop taking it. But when I lower the dose to sleep less I go weird; when I [increase] the dose (to the prescribed [level]) to be less weird I sleep too much and become depressed. To be honest my initial lowering of the dose was because I'm on weeklies and I felt too shit [awful] to pick up my prescription, so I eked it out.

Those are just the ones I remember; at various times I've also been on Risperidone and Valium for short bursts.

You may think, "Come off the drugs entirely". But you didn't see me before.

I started off as a la-de-da typical, textbook manic depressive. Years split down the middle with mania and depression, all mingled with psychosis. Then came the rapid cycling and the mixed episodes and my episodes were severe. Really bad. This, while not good, is better. I have . . . stopped self harming and mostly stopped throwing up. I do cope far better than I used to. I'm still mad, but not insane. I do think, and others agree, that I need the medication. For now, at least. It's doing half its job.

Seeking Stability

This year, I want to become at least stable enough to do something, anything, consistently. I don't see myself going back to work any time soon (not unless people are employing Shaky Twitchy Talkative Depressive Moody Midgets) but I want to do something. Right now, and for the past, oh, I don't know, forever, I can't sustain anything because my moods are so unstable that I get up the energy, which turns into raging agitation and paranoia then falls back into early-bed depression and complete silence. I try, but it's very hard. And once again it's beginning to f--- up my relationships. It's joyous. It's crazy, white-knuckle, rollicking fun. At the moment I am somewhere between depression and hypomania, of garbled thought that descends into paralysis then ascends again into nonsense and of wanting to run off somewhere, but getting the energy for the shops is difficult.

It's not conducive with, well, much. I just want, say, a month of doing something consistently. At least last year I was consistently suicidal. It was an achievement. Every day I woke up thinking, "Hell, I want to kill myself today. I wanted to kill myself two months ago. Is this what stability is like"?

I know I write, and that's something. I want to write more. Fiction, articles. I want to discipline myself and produce something beautiful and surprising. Tons of people are writers. To make a career out of it, you have to be talented, well connected and educated. I'm, er. Hm. And I want to learn something. Last year was such a dry, dead year. I'm taking the time to get better, but I want to be even better at being better. I want a future.

Do you think I have written things off too easily because of the side effects? I think I might have been too hasty and maybe there's something out there that will kill this enough for me to live my life somewhat. It's all I want, and by now, all I expect is a lessening of symptoms. No cure, no blank slate, just a little less. This is a little less but I have the feeling it is growing into something a little more. I'd like to push it in the opposite direction. Shrivel into insignificance. I'm not afraid of being "well". I don't worry about losing my identity—well, I do a little bit, since this is what I'm used to. But I realised that I'm a moody bint [naive woman] anyway.

When I look back, though, there's not much that seems worth trying again. I'm not being impatient. If I wanted instant gratification I would have said goodbye to medication and hello to alcohol about two years ago. I did the opposite.

Seroquel has been my main man for some time now, I'm very well aware of how it affects me. I don't want to be "fixed". I just want to be well enough for my life to not be consumed by manic depression, as it undoubtedly is right now. Medication is just stabilisers but at least when there were still options I felt like, if I fell, something could be done. Right now, there is the worrying absence of a safety net.

I'm not clamouring, "MORE MEDICATION! I LOVE IT! GIVE IT TO ME! I WANT TO BE DEPENDENT ON OTHER DRUGS TOO!", just reflecting on, "Christ, I've taken a lot. I thought I'd be smiling on the back of a book somewhere by now".

Doubts Remain

I really don't know where I'm going in terms of treatment. I'm continuing my appointments an' all but I feel stuck. It seems that if you're not trying to top yourself or trying to top someone else that it means you're magically all right. It's more insidious than that. I can have all the insight and entertaining asides in the world but this is still this.

But! I dragged myself to the glamourous surroundings of the [municipally administered] council gym earlier. It was in the morning. I don't do mornings thanks to Seroquel. I don't really do afternoons thanks to Seroquel. I'm very pale. Rob pulled me out of bed and I very dopily wandered to the station with him, adrift on my own little personal cloud. Then I drank two cups of coffee and tiptoed on the crosstrainer for ten minutes before getting a stitch [cramp]. I used to be able to pound it. It used to quiver beneath my #3 trainers and beg me for mercy. I've become so unfit. As soon as I was done I lit up a cigarette. I did walk to and from the gym so I got my thirty minutes of exercise a day, anyway. And I'm sure this killing cold (I don't have central heating and rely on a rather rubbish [useless] fan heater) is good for me. Bracing, as some would say. Though it's not a good sign when you have Thelma and Louise hair indoors.

Anyway, I like this, because it reminds me of those "well being" videos that depicted people like us as plebs [uneducated people] who watch too much Jeremy Kyle [British daytime talk show host] when we should be shiny haired and hosting dinner parties with Nescafé and f---ing salmon en croute or en route or whatever the name for fish in pastry is. And I watch TV online now so I don't have to sit through the adverts.

A Change in Diet
and Exercise Improved
My Bipolar Symptoms

Karl

In this account, the writer describes how he discovered he had bipolar disorder, and how changing his exercise and dietary habits lessened the effects of the once violent ups and downs.

From a very early age, I can remember being very agitated about some of the smallest things. What's important to a child can of course be nothing of consequence to an adult, but at the time I can remember asking questions that seemed very important to me. Are we late? Is there going to be anybody there? I would be seriously worried about the outcome of the answer to would it rain on school sports day? What would we do? Would it be cancelled? If it didn't rain, would everyone turn up? Did I look OK in my new sports strip [uniform]? Were we on time? Being late for an occasion opened the door to a whole new set of worries. This sort of worrying may not sound too extreme, but I was only five or six years old.

As far as I can remember, my parents—who 99% of the time were great, never picked up on my excessive anxiety. I always felt fobbed off with a half-baked answer to most of my questions. I honestly feel that if it had been spotted and helped by them, then things may have been easier for me as a child. I'm conscious with my own children today that children need lots of support and lots of love and reassurance from their parents.

One of the more unusual things I used to worry about in my teenage years was the weather. The weather, in particular

Karl, "My Personal Journey Through Depression," FightingDepression.co.uk, 2009. Reproduced by permission.

the wind, used to send shivers down my spine. It caused me to worry and fret about the slightest little thing. As an adult I've done a lot of reading, but have never come across this particular problem—I call it Weather Affective Disorder. It's a close cousin of Seasonal Affective Disorder or SAD, except that while SAD only affects people for a few months of the year, WAD affected me all year round. It could be wind, rain or even the blue sky that bothered me.

Despite my anxieties as a child, I was very good at sports and problem solving—I was also very creative.

The Start of the Bipolar

I joined the army when I was 16 and was happy to be involved in lots of sports and activities, but I found the constant change, lack of information and constantly living in fear of the unknown hard to cope with. Where was I to be sent next and when? Would I like it as much as what I was doing currently? I worried constantly.

After being in the army for about six years I had had enough of the constant change and upheaval, so I decided to leave and have a go at something else. I gave my one year's notice to leave. At that time the army had just made a lot of people redundant so I knew that I would still be sent out on active service in that year. Sure enough, I was sent to Northern Ireland on a six-month tour. On the whole that was a fun trip, and I had some good times with a good bunch of lads. After the six months we arrived back in our barracks in Germany to be told we had two weeks' leave, after which we were to prepare to go to Bosnia for another six-month tour of duty. At this point I was due to leave the army and was going to start my resettlement courses, so I was unhappy about this. This event seemed to act as a psychological trigger for me.

Our job in Bosnia was to build a runway so that NATO could launch air strikes if it needed to. When we arrived I knew something inside me was different, but still to this day I don't know what it was—I just didn't feel right. Our job was to build our own accommodation first, then to start on the runway. We started to build a tented camp the size of a small village, which resembled something from *MASH* [television show set in a military camp]. When we got there it was the . . . end of summer and very hot, and the working days were short and bearable (with the occasional visit to the beach thrown in). The showers we built were just cattle shed frames with water pumped into the hollow metal frame, then we punched a hole into the frame with a nail and there you had a shower. The toilet was one long trench dug into the floor, right next to the road so all the passing traffic could see you (most of the traffic was military).

After two months the summer had gone and the wet season was upon us, and this is when my life began to change forever. The days were wet, windy and dark. Our clothes were constantly wet, our tents had small rivers running through them and my sleeping bag and all my possessions were wet. It's impossible to describe the feeling of getting into a wet sleeping bag with water still dripping on you, the tent being blown over night after night in the torrential downpours. Getting up in the morning having not slept a wink all night due to being soaking wet was horrendous, everything was wet or extremely damp for three months. My morale was at an all-time low. Then a ray of light; our troop commander said that it was our turn for a bit of rest and recuperation. Just what the doctor ordered—or was it?

We were sent to a small hotel about 20 miles from camp, two single beds per room, en-suite [including a] shower and toilet, clean towels, dry clean beds, hot quality food, hot running water. It was heaven. To feel such comfort after such squalor was an amazing high[. W]ords cannot explain my elation.

For four whole days and nights we lived in relative luxury and ate good food. When the four days were up, we were bussed back to our tents. On the way back it started to dawn on me that I had left a very wet sleeping bag and clothes behind. When we arrived it was worse than I had expected. Whilst we were away the camp had been flooded and our tent was under a foot of water. I felt a terrible sinking feeling. It came over me suddenly; I just wanted to kill myself there and then. Life had no meaning at that point. I just burst into tears and sat there with my head in my hands wishing I was dead. As every second passed, I was going further down into a bottomless pit. I had been sitting there for what felt like hours when a medic came, picked me up and walked me to the tented medical centre.

That was the start of my bipolar life—a dizzying high followed by a catastrophic low. The treatment which followed was very basic, just a load of tablets to keep me quiet until I left the army in three months' time.

There followed two disastrously unsuccessful stays in two different psychiatric wards. I won't go into details just in case you need to have a short stay in one yourself. If you do, remember to never get angry, to keep smiling and telling them you're OK or your stay will be longer than you think. After this I resigned myself to self-diagnosis. I did a lot of reading and came to the fairly easy conclusion of bipolar disorder (manic depression), involving massive ups and massive downs.

Ten years later I had tried every antidepressant drug under the sun, none of which seemed to work for me—the side-effects were just as described in the leaflet, but the positive effects never materialised.

The Quest to Find Balance Begins

So after many failed treatments from the doctors, including herbal remedies, I decided to try and give my whole life and daily regime a good overhaul. This started with many hours of research to find the ultimate health plan, after these many hours of research they all led me to the same paths, which were general lifestyle, diet and exercise.

So I decided to make a plan to start exercising again. This was really easy as I was used to it from the Army, so I made a conscious effort to visit the gym at least 3–4 times per week. I was off to a great start, so no problem there.

The next thing that was really obvious was my diet. Wow, although I am relatively slim and in shape my diet was shocking so with the use of the Internet it is now really easy to research how to eat properly. . . . It went something like this:

- Swap black coffee with 2 sugars for Wulong tea (in fact I cut out almost all caffeine and only drank Wulong tea)

- Swap breakfast fry ups for Jordans luxury muesli [cereal] (except Sundays)

- Swap mid morning bacon buttie for a fruit salad (tough that one)

- Swap egg and chips [fried potatoes] for lunch for salad bowl and fruit

- Swap pie and chips for any lean protein with tons of any veg[etable] for evening meal

- No fizzy crap drinks, or flavoured water, just sparkling mineral water

- No alcohol mid week and only in moderation at the weekends

In fact I went as far as trying to reduce sugar in my diet to as low as possible. The same can be said for high carbohydrate food as well (Not that Atkins rubbish, just eating more lean protein). After doing all this I started to feel like things were really falling into place for me, and I began to feel a lot better. I don't know why but I still felt that one component was missing and it took me ages and ages to find out what it was.

So I kept a diary of my week's activities and food intake and showed it to a friend of mine who is a nutritionist. She took one look and was quite impressed, but she spotted right away that I had zero omega-3 in my diet at all!

The Omega-3 Hunt

So after sorting out my lifestyle my highs are now fairly manageable; they tend to upset those around me more than they upset me. As for the downs—I have them under control too.

After hearing that I was deficient in omega-3, I did some more research into what kinds of foods I needed to be eating to obtain this in my diet. Now apart from hemp seed, the only really natural food that is abundantly high in omega-3 is fish . . . . Noooo way, I can't stand fish! So I had to find an alternative to try and get this into my diet and the natural choice was fish oil supplements, as I was not prepared to eat fish! I went along to my local supermarket and bought some fish oil. I sat back and waited for my more balanced moods that everyone talks about regarding omega-3, but there was no change.

In the mean time I was given a book to read about the benefits of omega-3 fish oils, and about the benefits of something called EPA [eicosapentaenoic acid], an omega-3 nutrient. Having found a fish oil with a high EPA content, I again waited for the balance in mood to occur. Disappointed, I wondered if I was immune to fish oil, or if I still had the wrong type.

So I set about studying EPA fish oil in great depth, and what I found was to change my life.

I found that there are many grades of fish oil, from the old-fashioned cod liver oil right up to the Rolls Royce of fish oil—high-grade EPA concentrates. I searched for the highest grade of EPA that I could find. All the oils seemed to have unique selling points, but because of all the research I had done I could tell the hype from the truth. The biggest pointer

I was given was that oil, like alcohol, has strength, and that the quantity wasn't as important as the strength.

Again I searched for this elusive high-grade oil. It was apparent that all websites would use terms like 'high-grade' and 'ultra strong', which hampered my progress for genuine high grade oil. I eventually found a product that had some independent reviews and was allegedly one of the strongest oils available. I hoped this would be my solution, but again I felt no effect.

I rang the company involved and asked if I was doing something wrong, they asked how long I had been taking the oil for and how many capsules per day. They told me it was not a miracle cure, and that I would have to take four capsules per day for a minimum of three months for the oil to be fully absorbed. They also said that there were other things that could put the brakes on the absorption process, mainly your diet (I had this under control).

So I upped my dose to four caps in the morning and stayed with my good eating habits, trying to cut out all the rubbish. Four weeks later I started to notice some very strange things happening to me; I was behaving a little out of character. My anxiety levels about very stupid things had all but gone. I had stopped worrying about my car breaking down when it was raining, and about low-level fast-moving clouds. I also started to notice that my anger levels aimed at my children were also rapidly disappearing; I was talking to them rather than ranting at them. Not to mention the rapid growth of my hair and nails.

Over the following months I noticed many things starting to fall into place. My moods were more balanced than they had been for 15 years. I found myself laughing at comedy on the TV, which was not normal for me. I started not to care about little things, and I found it easier to let things go, whereas before they would nag at me for weeks on end. My concentration was nothing short of awesome, the ability to focus on a task was so much better, but the biggest thing had to be the balance of mood that this fish oil seemed to be giving me.

Absolutely 100% cured? No, but I am 95% better for having added it to my diet. If my old moods could be compared to a tidal wave, my moods now are gentle waves lapping on the shore, and they are very easy to manage.

I hope by writing about my experiences that something somewhere has fallen into place for someone else and that it may help.

The oil I am using at the moment is called PuraEpa. It's the strongest one I have found with an EPA concentration of 90% and contains no DHA (I found that some English Docs were suggesting there may be a competing mechanism between EPA and DHA) and it seems to be working very well. If I switch in the future I will post the details of why and what to do on this site.

I wish you all good luck.

Not All Children with Behavior Problems Need Medication

Laurel Williams

From her experience treating adolescents, the writer of the following selection concludes that many children are wrongly diagnosed with bipolar disorder. Misled by pharmaceutical ads and doctors who have insufficient insight into the patient's history, parents, she argues, too often demand medication for their children, hampering, not helping, the adolescents. Laurel L. Williams is program director of the Menninger Clinic's adolescent treatment program and assistant director of residency training, child and adolescent psychiatry. She is also assistant professor in the Menninger department of psychiatry and behavioral sciences at Baylor College of Medicine.

"I need these pills refilled," the weary mother says, displaying an array of empty bottles on the desk in my office. "My son is bipolar."

The boy, a quiet slip of a 10-year-old, had been prescribed two antipsychotics, two mood stabilizers, one antidepressant, two attention deficit disorder medications and another medication to manage the side effects of the antipsychotics.

The mother explained that she had just regained custody of her son and his brother. During the last year, while they were in foster care, a doctor had diagnosed the 10-year-old with bipolar disorder and attention deficit disorder and prescribed eight medications.

Laurel Williams, "Mental Health and Children," *Los Angeles Times*, December 14, 2008. Reproduced by permission.

Wrong Diagnosis

In the hour I spent with the boy and his mother, he exhibited no signs or symptoms of bipolar disorder, though he did display some irritability. In school, he continued to perform poorly in his second attempt at third grade. Both irritability and poor school performance can be significant problems. But I strongly questioned his diagnosis.

Bipolar disorder is a serious and devastating disease characterized by extreme changes in mood, thought, energy or behavior. How did Ronnie get labeled with such a potentially debilitating illness and prescribed eight powerful medications within such a short time span? Unfortunately, his case isn't unusual.

For a variety of reasons, bipolar diagnoses have become extremely popular. A Columbia University analysis of a National Center for Health Statistics survey found that the number of office visits for children diagnosed with bipolar disorder rose 40-fold between 1994 and 2003.

The reasons for the surge in bipolar diagnoses are complex. Despite advances in neuroscience, the brain, especially the developing brain, is still much of a mystery. More is unknown than known when it comes to effective treatment for children and adolescents with serious mental health problems. But that doesn't stop doctors and parents from desperately wanting to believe there are simple solutions, and what could be simpler than a pill?

Reasons Doctors May Overprescribe Medication

Since the 1980s, when pharmaceutical companies were granted permission to market their products directly to consumers, Americans have started believing that there is a drug to solve every discomfort and every mood. In my own practice, I've seen how determined parents can be to procure medication for their children that they have read about or seen advertised.

Meanwhile, pharmaceutical companies are paying inordinate sums of money to physicians to study their drugs. Doctors insist that they are not affected by the payments and that the research they do is pure, but it's hard to believe that the funding streams have no influence.

Another impetus to prescribe is the changing nature of medical practices. Physicians spend more time now than ever waiting on the phone, filling out paperwork and [going] through a labyrinth of regulations from insurance companies in order to be allowed the opportunity to treat their patients. Additionally, insurance companies, via their reimbursement plans, discourage healthcare providers from spending the time necessary to assess and treat childhood mental health problems. The average doctor's visit now wraps up in less than 15 minutes. It can be quicker and easier to medicate symptoms than to do a full assessment.

Even if doctors weren't short on time, the country is short on board-certified child and adolescent psychiatrists, the physicians best-trained to diagnose and treat child mental health problems. This shortage puts pressure on child psychiatrists to increase their patient loads, which then reduces the amount of time they can spend with individual patients.

Correct Diagnosis Takes Time

Adequately diagnosing psychiatric problems in a child requires multiple appointments and teamwork with the family, the school and the child. It requires a physician to stand up and say "no" to free gifts from drug companies and to critically review well-designed studies for appropriate assessment and treatment approaches. It requires our society to demand a healthcare system that affords access to appropriate levels of care, a system led by physicians who have demonstrated their commitment to the Hippocratic oath over financial gain. It requires the American people to take responsibility for their health and not expect pills to solve everything.

So what happened with the boy whose mother wanted me to refill his prescriptions? After an initial two-hour assessment at our clinic, he didn't return for his next appointment. When the clinic called to ask why, the boy's mother said that she had returned to his previous doctor. "Your doctor discriminated against me because I'm poor," she said, "and my son needs those pills for his bipolar."

Psychiatric assessment and treatment of a child can be hard. It often entails setting up educational testing to discover why he or she is failing in school, weekly individual and family therapy, and—sometimes—medication. I thought that my lengthy conversation with the boy's mother had convinced her that the above plan would actually provide her son with better care than refilling all eight medications at once.

Unfortunately, families often put more faith in what they see and hear in advertising than they do in physicians. As physicians, we need to win them back.

Thyroid Hormones Help Treat Bipolar Disorder

Peter Whybrow, interviewed by the Saturday Evening Post

In this interview, Peter Whybrow, M.D., discusses the benefits of using thyroid hormones to treat bipolar disorder. Thyroid hormones can shift the brain's physiological activity, which results in behavior changes that help bipolar patients recover from depression. Dr. Whybrow first discovered the link between bipolar disorder and the thyroid when he observed patients' strange behavior after being treated with thyroxine for thyroid carcinoma. Thyroid hormones are a promising treatment option for bipolar patients, but they are not yet a replacement for other mood-stabilizing drugs, and further study is required before the full impact of the hormone treatment is known.

Saturday Evening Post: Could you discuss your research into the link between thyroid function and bipolar disorder, particularly recent findings published in Molecular Psychiatry?

Dr. Peter Whybrow: The study is the most recent piece of a lot of work that attempts to understand how thyroid hormones modulate brain function and mood disorders. In this report specifically, how thyroid hormone may modify severe unremitting depression.

It has always intrigued me that people with severe hypothyroidism develop a syndrome that is very similar to depression, a finding that is historically well-known.

I first started studying the syndrome about 30 years ago. This recent study clearly shows that the addition of high-dose thyroxine in some individuals actually shifts the physiological activity in the brain, as measured by blood flow with positron emission tomography (PET) scans, to the areas which we know usually become active in recovery from depression. In these resistant depression patients, it mimics the same activity you see in other depressed individuals during recovery usually achieved just with antidepressant drugs.

The findings validate the idea that thyroid hormones have a powerful effect upon brain physiology. When that shift occurs in chronically depressed people, it associates with behavioral changes that we recognize as improvement in the depression.

Were you impressed with the results of the study, or did you anticipate improvements in the patients when you supplemented standard treatment with high-dose thyroid?

We anticipated the results because we've seen this happen many times before in our research over the past ten years. But the magnitude of the findings was very encouraging.

In the study, you administered supraphysiological doses of levothyroxine. What does "supraphysiological" mean, and what is an ordinary dose?

The doses that we have been using clinically lie between 0.2 and 0.4 rag, which produce blood levels of the hormone that are higher than the usual, hence the term "supraphysiological." My colleague in Germany, Michael Bauer, MD, PhD, who's the first author on the recent paper in *Molecular Psychiatry*, has used up to 0.5 rag, but we haven't done that in the U.S. These doses are much higher than ones used simply for thyroid hormone replacement in individuals with hypothyroidism or myxedema, usually following Hashimoto's disease, or secondary to the treatment of Grave's disease. But the doses are not quite as high as one might imagine from an historical viewpoint.

If you look through the scientific literature, you'll see that 25 to 30 years ago it was routine for individuals to be replaced with about double the dose they receive now. Most people today receive somewhere around 0.1 mg and 0.15 mg. Earlier, the doses given were in the 0.2 to 0.25 mg range. Thus, although we're using higher doses in our studies today, the fact is that they're not extraordinary. And certainly we've done extensive studies looking at bone metabolism, which, of course, every endocrinologist, including myself, worries about when administering thyroid hormone. I'm glad to say that we haven't found any significant shifts in bone metabolism, even in longitudinal studies of individuals who receive these doses.

Finding the Link Between Thyroid Problems and Bipolar Disorder

This may be a naive question, but are thyroid problems more common in certain forms of bipolar disorder, such as in mixed states or rapid cycling?

That's not a naive question at all. In fact, that is where the research into bipolar illness began. As background, I used to work for the Medical Research Council in London when I initially started this program. We treated thyroid carcinoma, and I was interested in the strange way in which people began to behave after we deprived them of thyroxine for about six months. This was in the early days when we didn't have triodothyronine to give them. From that, I began to look at thyroid hormone in relation to the treatment of depression, and I worked with Dr. Arthur Prange at the University of North Carolina to give doses of thyroid hormone—triodothyronine in this particular case—in association with antidepressant drugs. We found that the supplementation with thyroid hormone accelerated the activity of the antidepressant and people got better faster—a finding particularly true in women.

Fast-forward a decade or so and lithium became generally in use, which, of course, is an antithyroid agent as well as an antimanic agent. We along with others reported that thyroid disabilities had begun surfacing in people receiving lithium. In the late '80s, we studied a series of patients who had been given lithium and had an interesting syndrome now called rapid cycling disease, which is the most malignant form of bipolar disorder. As you know, manic-depressive illness, or bipolar disorder, is genetically predisposed, and there are several subtypes. Those individuals cycling extremely rapidly frequently had high levels of thyroid disability. Some studies show up to 50 percent with thyroid problems, but in our studies done at the University of Pennsylvania, we found about 20 to 25 percent had thyroid disease. Another fascinating observation was that almost all of those individuals who suffered this malignant form were women, usually premenopausal women.

Initially, we studied people only with abnormal thyroid indices in their peripheral blood. We discovered that actually we could manipulate mood in these severely ill people and that sometimes we could stop the cycling by administering high doses of thyroxine. Then later we found the same effect even in those patients who didn't have peripheral thyroid disease. So we began to develop the hypothesis, which eventually led to these brain imaging studies, that there might be some central brain-thyroid disability at work in rapid cycling disorder rather than a general thyroid problem. The brain controls its thyroid hormone rather precisely by deiodinazing—with a special deiodinase enzyme—the T4 to T3 on site. So we began to postulate that there might be some abnormality of the deiodinase or some other mechanism, such as thyroid receptor insensitivity in the brain. We have studied many of these possibilities over the years in various venues, and we found that, indeed, lithium does diminish deiodinase activity in the brain. We have also found that lithium changes the activity of some nuclear thyroid receptors in the brain.

If you put all that together, it suggests that there may be some people who are more vulnerable than others to the antithyroid effects of lithium. Even though they don't develop peripheral thyroid disease, they may be having some disability centrally, which would explain why it is that you can change the nature of their mood. Thus, in the case of rapid cycling, one can change the expression of the illness by giving high doses of thyroxine, even when peripheral thyroid metabolism appears to be normal.

Do you recommend that psychiatrists check thyroid function in bipolar patients?

One of the most important tests that I recommend to psychiatrists treating someone with manic-depressive illness who becomes resistant to lithium or other anticycling drugs, and develops a more malignant form of the illness, is a check of thyroid function.

Another thing that should be done because of this association between women and the cycling problem is to look at thyroid function in any young woman who has the rapid cycling illness. One possible explanation of why this occurs may lie in the competitive relationship between thyroid hormones and estrogens in the brain. Genetically, they share the same family of receptors, and these hormones tend to compete with each other. So if you are a premenopausal woman who has flushes of estrogen and progesterone driven by the monthly cycle, then if thyroid function diminishes for any reason, the competition tends to be won by the estrogens. This might be one of the destabilizing factors for young women with bipolar illness. Thus, the doctor should definitely check thyroid function in any female who has rapid cycling, measuring thyroid stimulating hormone (TSH) to see whether it's elevated at all.

Particulars of the Study

In your seven-week study, you utilized four doses of the level of thyroxine. Did any particular dose appear to be most effective?

We escalated the doses to give ultimately a high level of circulating thyroxine, so those doses were just the way in which we paced the escalation. For four weeks or so, we maintained patients at the levels that in our experience are therapeutic for individuals with severe resistant depression.

Did participants in the study remain on mood-stabilizing drugs?

Yes. We've learned over the years that because these people are so sick, very often taking them off their medications is unethical. Their illness gets worse. Thus, we stabilize their medications, then we add in the thyroxine as an independent variable.

Why did your study include only menopausal or premenopausal women between 18 and 55 and not include, for example, senior patients?

The reason we constrained it 18 to 55 is because we were looking particularly in this group of patients who had vulnerability. The answer to your other question is that you have to be careful when using these medications. Obviously, we always review very carefully cardiovascular disease or any other disorder that we would be concerned about in regard to the use of thyroid hormone. As age increases, you have to worry about bone metabolism and cardiovascular function when using high doses of thyroid medication.

One interesting thing we have discovered is that when we give individuals with severe depression or rapid cycling high-dose thyroxine, they do not respond in the same way as would, let's say, "normal" people respond to thyroid hormone. If you give somebody without illness increasing amounts of thyroid hormone, then after a certain dose they begin to feel very anxious and distressed. For reasons we don't yet understand, this doesn't occur in rapid cycling or resistant depression patients. Very often they tolerate high doses without any side effects whatsoever. They don't experience changes in blood pressure, sweating, or anxiety. The pulse rate goes up a little bit, but not much, which also suggests that they have some sort of physiological difference.

Up to age 55, we feel fairly confident that high-dose thyroxine therapy is not going to harm anybody, but above that age level, we are much more cautious.

And there are other caveats. First, those who come to us usually do so after they've tried many, many other things. Most are suffering badly, either with chronic malignant depression or rapid cycling—both of which are very miserable illnesses to live with, believe me.

One must think of the issue in terms of physiological costs versus benefits. Most patients have come to the end of a long list of treatments before they receive high-dose thyroxine. And the good news is that some patients do extraordinarily well—with almost magical improvement.

Your report mentioned a decrease in systolic blood pressure. Wouldn't that be a plus for geriatric patients with bipolar and hypertension?

It would be, yes. But again one has to be cautious, because if patients do have cardiovascular problems, one doesn't want to jump in too enthusiastically without appropriate assessment.

In your study, you used levothyroxine, which consists of synthetic T4—the generic form of thyroxine. How does this compare with Armour Thyroid tablets, which include T3 and T4?

In our studies, we've always used thyroxine because it's physiologically much more easily tracked. We want to be able to find out what is happening to the levels of T4 and also to the thyroid stimulating hormone (TSH). If you give T3, which has a much shorter half-life, it confuses the situation, because it switches off T4 production in the indigenous gland. In general, it's not as clean as a physiological experiment. Armour Thyroid tends to have both T3 and T4 in there. Although it's pretty well stabilized, there is some variation between the T3 and T4 percentages.

Therapeutically, do they have the same benefit?

Yes. Whether it's synthetically produced or from a sheep's gland, thyroxine is exactly the same molecule.

Are you familiar with psychiatrists in the United States who are using thyroid medications to treat bipolar depression?

There are many individuals. I can't give you a list. But many psychiatrists who care for a large number of severely ill bipolar people eventually explore the use of thyroid hormone as one possible solution to their patients' difficulties. . . .

You mentioned earlier your collaboration with researchers in Germany. Is the therapy utilized more commonly in Europe or elsewhere?

Yes. In fact, Dr. Bauer has done an enormous amount of work in Berlin. We have collaborated for probably about eight years now. He was actually here at UCLA's Neuropsychiatric Institute for a couple of years and he was the leader on the study recently published in *Molecular Psychiatry*. Dr. Bauer also has ongoing studies in Germany, and two or three different universities in Europe.

Would you envision this research expanding in the United States?

Many universities use this. There aren't too many that have formal programs in thyroid and depression. For some reason, it has not been of as much interest in the United States as has the study of steroids and depression. But as I mentioned, there are many individual practitioners who are familiar with these ideas and use them around the country. But there aren't as many organized research programs as you might imagine.

In your recent paper, why did you mention right-handedness?

When you're doing a brain study, the handedness makes a difference in terms of the way blood flow distributes itself, so the dominant hemisphere needs to be the same in each patient. We chose handedness as a simple way of measuring dominance.

In your imaging scans, the positron emission tomography scans were simply to follow brain metabolism?

Exactly.

In the study published in Molecular Psychiatry, *could you discuss the imaging studies that demonstrated the altered brain activity?*

We were measuring the shifts in blood flow as reflected by the glucose utilization in the brain.

In these severely depressed patients, we found that the distribution of blood flow was very similar to that of other reports in the literature, when scanned by the same technique. Crudely put, the limbic structures tend to be active and the frontal lobes tend to be inactive, a finding that reverses when the depression is treated. We witnessed that shift in our patients as well. The only difference is that our patients had already been treated very energetically with antidepressants and had not responded in the typical way. It was as if the abnormal distribution of blood flow persisted, even though they received what is considered adequate intervention for depression.

Future Studies

What role do you think that your research will play in the future treatment with bipolar and rapid cycling? Do you think it will integrate into the therapy?

Yes, eventually. In some ways, what we're seeing is similar to the use of steroids as a pharmacologic agent (as opposed to an endocrine agent) in the treatment of conditions like acute asthma or chronic inflammatory disease and so forth.

The goal of future studies is to become more sophisticated in understanding the central mechanisms that are impaired in these individuals who don't get better when given the usual therapeutic agents but who nonetheless are triggered into improvement through the use of thyroid hormone. We must now investigate potential genetic differences within the receptors and the neurochemical pathways that are influenced by thyroid hormones.

Dr. Bauer has been talking with some scientists in Scandinavia about looking at potential genetic variance and possible syndromes of thyroid receptor resistance in these patients. It may well be that in the long run, we'll discover something that will circumvent the need for the use of thyroid hormone, because the thyroid hormone may be just the mechanism that "un-sticks" the system, in the same way as eventually we might find something that will turn off the inflammatory action in the person with severe asthma.

Do you have any suspicions about other potential causative agents, such as viral agents, in rapid cycling and bipolar disorder?

My own sense is that bipolar disorder is one of the diseases predisposed by genetics. The fascinating thing about bipolar disease in general—not just about the link between bipolar disease and thyroid disease—is that bipolar illness is heavily influenced by familial and therefore genetic inheritance. Four or five different areas in the genome now seem to be shaping up for possible sites where abnormalities or aberrations of genetic accounting occur in bipolar disorder. These sites vary from study to study, suggesting that bipolar illness is a complex trait. Not all the genes may be aberrant genes, but rather, they are aberrant in combination. There is no unique gene as, for example, the Huntington's gene. In bipolar illness, we may discover just variations of genes that are very important and useful in what they usually do. It may well be that's why you find in families with bipolar disorder: a disturbance of emotional and social behavior, others who seem to be very emotionally and socially adept. You get this interesting matrix of people, some of whom are extremely talented and rewarded in our social structure while other family members with just a slight genetic variation have too much energy until they surge over the top and collapse into the asylum. Probably these variants of genetic composition are not driven by viral illness, although that may be so in schizophrenia and other illnesses where structural abnormalities early in life express themselves later during maturation and adolescence.

Could you share new treatments for rapid cycling and other forms of bipolar disorder in the pipeline?

What manic-depressive illness and schizophrenia have in common is that both respond in the acute phases to dopamine-blocking drugs. The new dopamine-blocking drugs, introduced mainly for schizophrenia, also work in severely ill bipolar patients. Another area for long-term control, which shows mixed promise, is the use of agents used in the treatment of epilepsy. One way of conceptualizing manic-depressive disease is as a disorder with a radically different time course but nonetheless sharing some similarities with epilepsy, where focal firing oscillates with quiescence.

Would those agents include neurontin (gabapentin) and lamictal (lamotrigine)?

Yes, that's right.

We have written about Dr. Andrew Stoll's research at Harvard on the use of omega-3s. What do you think about the potential of omega-3s?

It is empirical evidence in the same way that the thyroid research is empirical, but Dr. Stoll seems to get positive results that make a clinical difference. We know that omega-3 fatty acids are particularly important in the central nervous system, so the theory has logic behind it. Omega-3 supplementation is a treatment, like thyroid, which we need to explore and follow carefully. I would not throw out without research any potential agents for these individuals because they suffer so badly.

Organizations to Contact

The editors have compiled the following list of organizations concerned with the issues debated in this book. The descriptions are derived from materials provided by the organizations. All have publications or information available for interested readers. The list was compiled on the date of publication of the present volume; information provided here may change. Be aware that many organizations take several weeks or longer to respond to inquiries, so allow as much time as possible.

Alternative Medicine Foundation (AMF)
PO Box 60016, Potomac, MD   20859
(301) 340-1960 • fax: (301) 340-1936
Web site: www.amfoundation.org

The Alternative Medicine Foundation is a nonprofit organization that seeks to provide responsible and reliable information about alternative medicine to the public and health professionals. Its Web site features a resource guide and a searchable guide on herbal medications such as St. John's wort.

American Academy of Child and Adolescent Psychiatry (AACAP)
3615 Wisconsin Ave. NW, Washington, DC   20016-3007
(202) 966-7300 • fax: (202) 966-2891
Web site: www.aacap.org

The American Academy of Child and Adolescent Psychiatry is a national professional medical association dedicated to treating and improving the quality of life for children, adolescents, and families affected by psychiatric disorders. The AACAP publishes interviews and videos on its Web site, as well as the information series *Facts for Families*.

American Psychological Association (APA)
750 First Street NE, Washington, DC   20002-4242
(800) 374-2721 • fax: (202) 336-5708
e-mail: public.affairs@apa.org
Web site: www.apa.org

The American Psychological association is the world's largest organization of psychologists. It publishes numerous books, journals, and videos, and offers information on depression treatment and psychotherapy on its Web site.

BPHope.com
374 Delaware Ave., Buffalo, NY   14202
Phone: (716) 614-HOPE (4673) • fax: (716) 614-4676
Web site: www.bphope.com

BPHope is a Web site offering a multitude of resources for the bipolar community. Its publication *BP Magazine*'s primary purpose is to create community among people living with bipolar disorder.

Center for Mental Health Services
PO Box 2345, Rockville, MD   20847
(800) 789-2647 • fax: (240) 221-4295
Web site: www.mentalhealth.org

The Substance Abuse and Mental Health Services Administration's (SAMHSA) National Mental Health Information Center provides information about mental health via telephone, its Web site, and more than 600 publications.

Child and Adolescent Bipolar Foundation
820 Davis Street, Suite 520, Evanston, IL   60201
(847) 492-8510
e-mail: cabf@bpkids.org
Web site: www.bpkids.org

The Child and Adolescent Bipolar Foundation seeks to improve the lives of families raising children and teens living with bipolar disorder and related conditions. It offers articles and a learning center online.

Depression and Bipolar Support Alliance (DBSA)
730 N. Franklin Street, Suite 501, Chicago, IL   60654-7225
(800) 826-3632 • fax: (312) 642-7243
Web site: www.dbsalliance.org

The Depression and Bipolar Support Alliance is a patient-directed nonprofit organization focusing on the most prevalent mental illnesses. The organization fosters an environment of understanding about the impact and management of these life-threatening illnesses by providing up-to-date, scientifically based tools and information. Articles and brochures are available on the organization's Web site.

International Foundation for Research and Education on Depression
PO Box 17598, Baltimore, MD   21297-1598
(410) 268-0044 • fax: (443) 782-0739
e-mail: info@ifred.org
Web site: www.ifred.org

The International Foundation for Research and Education on Depression (iFred), is a nonprofit organization dedicated to helping research the causes of depression, to support those dealing with depression, and to combat the stigma associated with depression. The foundation offers a variety of articles and resources through its Web site.

MedlinePlus National Library of Medicine/National Institutes of Health
8600 Rockville Pike, Bethesda, MD   20894
e-mail: custserv@nlm.nih.gov
Web site: www.nlm.nih.gov/medlineplus

MedlinePlus directs people to information to help answer health questions. MedlinePlus brings together authoritative information from National Library of Medicine, the National Institutes of Health (NIH), and other government agencies and health-related organizations. MedlinePlus also has extensive information about drugs, an illustrated medical encyclopedia, interactive patient tutorials, and latest health news.

125

Mental Health America
2000 N. Beauregard Street, 6th Floor, Alexandria, VA   22311
(703) 684-7722 • fax: (703) 684-5968
Web site: www.nmha.org

Mental Health America (formerly known as the National Mental Health Association) is a national nonprofit organization dedicated to helping people live mentally healthier lives. It publishes resource guides and wellness tips on its Web site.

National Alliance on Mental Illness (NAMI)
2107 Wilson Blvd., Suite 300, Arlington, VA   22201-3042
(703) 524-7600 • fax: (703) 524-9094
Web site: www.nami.org

The National Alliance on Mental Illness is the nation's largest grassroots mental health organization and seeks to improve the lives of individuals and families affected by mental illness. Founded in 1979, NAMI has affiliates in every state and in more than 1,100 communities across the country. It provides articles and interviews online.

National Institute of Mental Health (NIMH)
Science Writing, Press, and Dissemination Branch
Bethesda, MD   20892-9663
(301) 443-4513 • fax: (301) 443-4279
e-mail: nimhinfo@nih.gov
Web site: www.nimh.nih.gov

The mission of the National Institute of Mental Health is to transform the understanding and treatment of mental illnesses through basic and clinical research, paving the way for prevention, recovery, and cure. It makes articles and information about mental illness, as well as the magazine *Science News*, available online.

For Further Research

Books

Andy Behrman, *Electroboy: A Memoir of Mania*. New York: Random House, 2002.

Lesley Berk, *Living with Bipolar*. London: Vermilion, 2009.

Lana Castle, *Finding Your Bipolar Muse: How to Master Depressive Thoughts and Manic Floods and Access Your Creative Power*. Cambridge, MA: Da Capo, 2006.

Benjamin Diven, *Closing the Chasm: Letters from a Bipolar Physician to His Son*. iUniverse.com, 2009.

Pete Earley, *Crazy*. New York: G.P. Putnam's Sons, 2006.

Judy Eron, *What Goes Up . . . Surviving the Manic Episode of a Loved One*. Fort Lee, NJ: Barricade Books, 2005.

Kerrie Eyers and Gordon Parker, eds., *Mastering Bipolar Disorder: An Insider's Guide to Managing Mood Swings and Finding Balance*. St. Leonards, Australia: Allen & Unwin, 2008.

Gianni L. Faedda and Nancy Austi, *Parenting a Bipolar Child: What to Do and Why*, Oakland, CA: New Harbinger, 2006.

Julie Fast, *Take Charge of Bipolar Disorder: A Four-Step Plan for You and Your Loved Ones to Manage the Illness and Create Lasting Stability*. New York: Warner Wellness, 2006.

Ellen Frank, *Treating Bipolar Disorder: A Clinician's Guide to Interpersonal and Social Rhythm Therapy*. New York: Guilford Press, 2005.

Barbara Geller and Melissa DelBello, *Bipolar Disorder in Childhood and Early Adolescence*. New York: Guilford Press, 2003.

Rosalie Greenberg, *Bipolar Kids: Helping Your Child Find the Calm in the Mood Storm*. Cambridge, MA: Da Capo Life Long, 2007.

Gail Griffith, *Will's Choice: A Suicidal Teen, a Desperate Mother, and a Chronicle of Recovery*. New York: Harper-Collins, 2005.

Craig Hamilton and Neil Jameson, *Broken Open*. New York: Bantam Books, 2004.

Marya Hornbacher, *Madness: A Bipolar Life*. New York: Houghton Mifflin, 2008.

Sheri Johnson and Robert Leahy, *Psychological Treatment of Bipolar Disorder*. New York: Guilford Press, 2004.

David Lovelace, *Scattershot: My Bipolar Family*. New York: Dutton Adult, 2008.

Christopher Lukas, *Blue Genes: A Memoir of Loss and Survival*. New York: Doubleday, 2008.

John McManamy, *Living Well with Depression and Bipolar Disorder: What Your Doctor Doesn't Tell You . . . That You Need to Know*. New York: Collins, 2006.

David Miklowitz, *The Bipolar Teen: What You Can Do to Help Your Child and Your Family*. New York: Guilford Press, 2007.

Francis Mark Mondimore, *Bipolar Disorder: A Guide for Patients and Families*, 2nd ed. Baltimore: Johns Hopkins University Press, 2006.

Jay Neugeboren, *Imagining Robert: My Brother, Madness and Survival*. Piscataway, NJ: Rutgers University Press, 2003.

Demitri Papolos and Janice Papolos, *The Bipolar Child: The Definitive and Reassuring Guide to Childhood's Most Misunderstood Disorder*, 3rd ed. New York: Broadway Books, 2006.

Gordon Parker, *Bipolar II Disorder: Modeling, Measuring and Managing*. Cambridge University Press, 2009.

Jane Pauley, *Skywriting: A Life Out of the Blue*. New York: Random House, 2004.

Lizzie Simon, *Detour: My Bipolar Road Trip in 4-D*. New York: Washington Square Press, 2003.

Mary Worthen, *Journey Not Chosen . . . Destination Not Known: Living with Bipolar Disorder*. Little Rock, AR: August House, 2001.

Periodicals

B. Bower, "Bipolar Surprise: Mood Disorder Endures Antidepressant Setback," *Science News*, March 31, 2007.

Benedict Carey, "Youth, Meds, and Suicide," *Los Angeles Times*, February 2, 2004.

John Cloud, "When Sadness Is a Good Thing," *Time*, August 16, 2007.

Helen Davis Gardner, "Don't Let Bipolar Disorder Ruin Your Relationships and Your Life: With Treatment, You Can Live a Successful and Fulfilling Life," *Ebony*, April 2008.

The Daily Mail (London), "Kerry Looks for Cure in the Priory; Bipolar Disorder: Troubled Kerry Katona," July 20, 2007.

The Daily Mail (London), "High-Tech Vest Can Diagnose Mental Illness," June 12, 2007.

Richard DeGrandpre, "Trouble in Prozac Nation," *Nation*, January 5, 2004.

Evening Chronicle (Newcastle, England), "Every Day I Would Ask 'Are You Going to Kill Yourself?'" August 10, 2006.

The Evening Standard (London), "Let's Give Britney a Break," January 8, 2008.

Kenneth Fox, "Monster in Our Midst: Living with Bipolar Disorder," *World and I*, February 2004.

E. Jaffe, "Deadly Disorder: Imagined-Ugliness Illness Yields High Suicide Rate," *Science News*, July 22, 2006.

Joshua Kendall, "Talking Back to Prozac," *Boston Globe*, February 1, 2004.

The Mail on Sunday (London), "Revealed: Why Sophie Has Epic Highs and Lows," September 10, 2006.

The Mirror (London), "TV Shrink: Britney Needs Urgent Help; Fears for Star over Bipolar Illness as She Hides out with Snapper Friend," January 7, 2008.

Tina Hesman Saey, "Body and Brain: Possible Link Between Inflammation and Bipolar Disorder," *Science News*, April 12, 2008.

South Wales Echo (Cardiff, Wales), "Cardiff Research May Help Spell Relief for Thousands of Bipolar Sufferers; University Scientists Identity Key Genes Behind Disorder," August 19, 2008.

Susan Stevens, "Diagnosis of Bipolar Disorder Is Rising, Particularly in Children," *Daily Herald* (Arlington Heights, IL), September 27, 2004.

Susan Stevens, "Highs and Lows: A Common Medication Triggered Jane Pauley's Bipolar Disorder. Could It Happen to You?" *Daily Herald* (Arlington Heights, IL), September 27, 2004.

Sunday Mercury (Birmingham, England), "Your Life: Is There a Cure for My Mood Swings?" May 7, 2006.

E. Fuller Torrey, "Bird Brains," *Washington Monthly*, May 2001.

Washington Times, "'It's a Hidden Epidemic'; Diagnoses of Bipolar Disorder on Rise among Youngsters," March 9, 2005.

Washington Times, "Bipolar Disorder," May 20, 2002.

Index

A

Aarons, Becky, 59–61
Abilify (medication), 88
Ablow, Keith, 89
Acceptance of having bipolar disorder, 53–54
Agitation, 33, 34
Allergies, 20
Antidepressant medications, 30, 103, 108
Antipsychotic medications, 30, 49
Anxiety, 51
Art therapy, 83
Attention-deficit/hyperactivity disorder (ADHD), 72, 108

B

Bauer, Michael, 113, 119
Bipolar Central (Web site), 90
Bipolar disorder
    admission of in dating, 85
    caricature of, 87
    coming to terms with, 46–52
    as a criminal defense, 88–89
    fatal aspects of, 30
    genetic inheritance of, 63–64, 121–122
    Harvard University research, 122
    lack of diagnosis of, 80
    mixed state symptoms, 19
    onset of (patient's story), 102–103
    Patrick Jamieson story, 16–27
    postpartum psychosis and, 41–45
    racing thoughts in, 18–19
    regrets from having, 52
    religion (Jewish) and, 72–78
    sense of despair from, 53–57
    up-and-down behavior, 53–57
    See also Hospitalization; Medications; Symptoms of bipolar disorder; Treatments (non-pharmacological)
Bipolar disorder, types I and II, 81
Bipolar disorder NOS (not otherwise specified), 33
Blair, Jayson, 88
Blogs about bipolar disorder, 89–90
Blood testing, 22
Borderline personality disorder, 32, 33, 37
Brain research
    on adults, 67
    chemistry imbalances, 120
    on children, 72–73
    genes and, 13–14
    PET scans, 113
Brain Research Success Stories (Society for Neuroscience), 13

C

Carbamazepine (medication), 95
Caricature of bipolar disorder, 87
Chase's Law (2006), 14
Children
    of bipolar parents, 65, 67, 68–69
    fear of mental illness, 70–71
    misdiagnosis of, 108–111

Children with bipolar disorder, 70–78
    brain chemistry imbalances, 72–73
    hospitalization of, 73–74
    infancy, 71
    school problems, 71–72
    suicide threats, 75–76
    violent behavior, 71
Christman, Ryan, 53–57
Clark, Justin, 85–93
Client-psychiatrist relationship, 26–27
Codependency, 65
Cognitive behavior therapy, 30
Compliance with treatments, 30
Cortisone-based inhalant, 16–17
Couples (marriage) with bipolar disorder, 62–69, 79–85
Crisis Response Center, 35
Crying spells, 48–49, 51
Cutting behaviors (of self), 33–38

D

Dating a person with bipolar disorder, 85–93
Delusional behavior, 64
Depersonalization, 34
Depression
    brain chemistry basis, 14
    darkness of, 63–64
    excessive sleeping from, 32–33, 63
    hospitalization for, 32–40
    mania as precursor of, 19
    onset of, 18
    postpartum depression, 41–45
    self-medication for, 21
    suicidal ideation/behaviors, 22, 86

triggers of, 17
    See also Jamieson, Patrick
De Rosnay, Joel, 55
Despair, 53–57
DHA (in omega-3 fatty acids), 107
Diet and exercise, 100–108
    food exchanges, 104
    mood stabilization from, 106–107
    omega-3 fatty acids, 105–107, 122
Disease-based courtship and romance, 79–84, 85–93
Disorganization of life, 88
Divorce, 21, 50, 67–68, 83–84
Doctor-patient relationships, 67–68
Dopamine-blocking drugs, 122
DSM-IV (Diagnostic and Statistical Manual of Mental Disorders), 87
Duke, Patty, 46–52
    childhood struggles, 47–48
    depression/mania episodes, 48–50
    entertainment career success, 46–49, 51
    life-saving diagnosis, 51–52
    medication treatment, 48–49

E

Eccentric behavior, 17
Edwards, Chase, 12, 14
Electroshock therapy, 66
EPA (eicosapentaenoic acid), 105–106, 107
Epstein-Barr syndrome, 20, 23

F

Father (parent) with bipolar disorder, 59–61
Fish oil supplements (for omega-3 fatty acids), 105–107, 122
Focusing difficulties, 20
Fox, Kenneth Richard, 62–69
Friendships, loss of, 65–66

G

Garrett Lee Smith Memorial Act, 14
Gavin, Kara, 12, 14
Generalized anxiety disorder (GAD), 33
Genetic inheritance, 63–64, 121–122
Gen-X, 80
Grave's disease, 113

H

Halfway houses, 55–56
Hanging, 61, 75–76
Harvard University, bipolar research, 122
Hashimoto's disease, 113
Health insurance, 25, 27
Hiding symptoms, 66
High (rapid) cycling, 20–21, 122
High functioning patients, 37–39
Hong, Y. Euny, 79–84
Hospitalization
   after a suicide attempt, 82–83
   as inpatient, 24, 33–36, 38–39
   of child with bipolar, 73–74
   for loss of consciousness, 91–92
   medication adjustments, 40
   for medication failures, 59
   partial programs, 36
   of Patty Duke, 50
   for postpartum depression, 43–44
   psychiatric interview, 36–37
   for self-injury, 33–36
   voluntary admission, 40
Hyperconfidence, 80
Hypersexual activity, 66
Hypochondria, 23
Hypomania, 29–30, 37, 90, 97

I

Immaturity, 80
Impulsive behaviors, 33, 36
Individualism, 17
Inheritance of bipolar disorder, 63–64, 121–122
Inpatient hospitalization, 24, 33–36, 35, 38–39
Insomnia, 32–33, 44, 66

J

Jamieson, Patrick
   asthma treatment ill effects, 16–17
   family move to Philadelphia, 22–23
   family move to Texas, 17–18
   family suicide, 21–22
   high (rapid) cycling, 20–21
   initial manic episode, 16
   mixed state symptoms, 19
   onset of depression, 18
   racing thoughts, 18–19
   on stereotypes of mental illness, 23–25
   treatment struggles, 25–26
   verbal aggressiveness, 2

Jamison, Kay, 87
Judaism and bipolar disorder, 72–78

K

Keller, Helen, 46
King, Cheryl, 14

L

LaFave, Debra, 88
Lamictal (medication), 42–43, 95
Lithium (medication), 20–21, 31, 51, 94, 114
Loved ones with bipolar disorder
    child, 70–78
    dating, 85–93
    father, 59–61
    married couples, 62–69, 79–85
    siblings, 64
    wife, 62–69
Low functioning patients, 36

M

Mania symptoms
    agitations, 34
    described, 19–20
    erratic behaviors, 83–84
    hypomania, 29–30, 37, 90, 97
    medication for, 21
    as normal life, 80
    spending money, 80–81
Manic depression. *See* Bipolar disorder
Manic irritability, 34
Married couples with bipolar disorder, 62–69, 79–85
Medical Research Council (England), 114

Medications
    Abilify, 88
    antidepressants, 30, 103, 108
    antipsychotics, 30, 49
    Carbamazepine, 95
    for depression, 21
    Lamictal, 42–43, 95
    Lithium, 20–21, 31, 51, 94, 114–116
    for mania symptoms, 21
    mood stabilizers, 108
    overprescription of, 109–110
    for postpartum depression, 42
    Risperidone, 96
    Seroquel, 96, 98
    side effects from, 31, 73, 94–99
    Stelazine, 48
    Thorazine, 48
    thyroid hormones, 112–122
    Valium, 96
    Zopiclone, 94–95
    Zyprexa, 42–43, 88, 95
    See also Treatments (non-pharmacological)
Menninger Clinic, 108
Mental illness
    high functioning patients, 37–39
    stereotypes of, 23–25
    stigma of, 23–24, 31, 37–38
The Miracle Worker (play and film), 48
Misdiagnosis of children, 108–111
Mixed state symptoms, 19, 33
Molecular Psychiatry (journal), 113, 119
Money spending behaviors, 80–81
Mononucleosis, 19–20
Mood stabilizers, 108
Mood swings, 33, 42, 59, 95

N

National Institute of Mental Health, 27
National Mental Health Association, 88

O

Obsessive-compulsive behavior, 88
Oliver, David, 90
Omega-3 fatty acids, 105–107, 122
Orkin, Debbie, 70–78
Overprescription of medications, 109–110
Overspending, 66
Overworking, 66

P

Paranoia, 64
Parents with bipolar disorder, 59–61
Partial hospitalization programs, 36
The Patty Duke Show (TV show), 48–49
Pauley, Jane
    bipolar diagnosis, 28–29
    depression symptoms, 29
    hypomania symptoms, 29–30
Pearce, Anna, 46–52
Perry, Patrick, 28–31
PET (positron emission tomography) brain scans, 113
Pharmacological alternatives, 31
Postpartum depression, 41–45, 64
Prange, Arthur, 114
Pseudosupport for patients, 66
Psychiatric interview, 36–37, 74–75

Psychology Today (magazine), 89
Psychosocial interventions, 27
Psychotherapy
    for postpartum depression, 44–45
    for spouses/family members, 65
    usefulness of, 30, 36
    See also Support groups

R

Rapid cycling, 20–21, 120, 122
Rebound effect, 30
Relapse, 65–66
Risperidone (medication), 96
Roller coaster behavior, 53–57, 60–61, 65
Romance, 79–84, 85–93

S

Safety net for the public, 67–69
Scanlon, Matt, 46–52
Schizophrenia, 23, 38, 122
Seasonal Affective Disorder (SAD), 101
Self-confidence, loss of, 65
Self-destructive behaviors
    cutting, 33–38
    hanging (by the neck), 61, 75–76
    urges for, 39–40
Self-help books, 91
Self-indulgent hypochondria, 23
Self-reflection, 26
Seroquel (medication), 96, 98
Shopping, 35
Short-term therapy, 40
Siblings with bipolar disorder, 64

Side effects from medications, 31, 73, 94–99

Skill-based therapy, 40

Skywriting: A Life Out of the Blue (Pauley), 28–29, 30

Sleeping, excessive, 32–33, 63

Sleeping pill overdose, 81–82

Sleeplessness (insomnia), 20, 32–33, 44, 66

Smith, Garrett, 12–13

Social Anxiety and Bipolar Diary of Annie blog, 89–90

Society for Neuroscience, 13

Spears, Britney, 89

Spending money, 80–81

Spouses with bipolar disorder, 79–85

Stelazine (medication), 48

Stereotypes of mental illness, 23–25

Stigma of mental illness, 23–24, 31, 37–38

Stoll, Andrew, 122

Suicidal ideation/behaviors
  of children, 75–76
  depression leading to, 86
  overdosing of sleeping pills, 81–82
  in postpartum depression, 42, 64
  repeated attempts, 84
  self-destructiveness and, 33–34, 37

Support groups
  for borderline personality disorder, 37
  for parents, 77
  for spouses, 65
  See also Psychotherapy

The Symbiotic Man (De Rosnay), 55

Symptoms of bipolar disorder
  anger, 65
  disorganization, 88
  excessive sleeping, 32–33, 63
  high (rapid) cycling, 20–21, 120, 122
  hyperconfidence, 80
  hypomania, 29–30, 37
  insomnia, 32–33, 44, 66
  mixed states, 19
  racing thoughts, 18–19
  spending money, 80–81
  up-and-down behavior, 53–57, 60–61, 65
  verbal aggressiveness, 22
  violent behavior, 62, 66, 67

T

Teenagers
  bipolar diagnosis of, 16–27
  with bipolar parent, 59–61

Thinking/racing thoughts, 18–19

Thorazine (medication), 48

Thyroid hormone treatment, 112–122

Thyroid malfunction, 22

Tranquilizers and suicide ideation, 34

Treatments (non-pharmacological), 13
  art therapy, 83
  compliance irregularities, 30
  diet and exercise, 100–108
  overcorrections, 66
  psychosocial interventions, 27
  psychotherapy, 30, 36, 44–45, 65
  short-term therapy, 40
  structured environments, 34

struggles with, 25–26
unsuccessful/incomplete, 67–68
See also Hospitalization; Medications
Trudeau, Garry, 28
Types I and II bipolar disorder, 81

U

UCLA Neuropsychiatric Institute, 119
Unipolar depression, 30
An Unquiet Mind (Jamison), 87
Up-and-down behavior, 53–57, 60–61, 65

V

Valium (medication), 96
Violent behavior
of adult, 62, 66, 67
of child, 71–72

W

Washington Post (newspaper), 13
Weather Affective Disorder, 101
Weird Cake blog, 89
Whybrow, Peter, 112–122
Wife with bipolar disorder, 62–69
Williams, Laurel, 108–111
Winfrey, Oprah, 89

Y

Youth Depression and Suicide Prevention Program, 14
Youth Guidance Center, 23

Z

Zopiclone (medication), 94
Zyprexa (medication), 42–43, 88, 95